Listen to the Men!...
THINK for YOURSELF

Listen to the Men!...
THINK for YOURSELF

Ron E. Jefferson

authorHOUSE®

AuthorHouse™
1663 Liberty Drive
Bloomington, IN 47403
www.authorhouse.com
Phone: 1 (800) 839-8640

© 2015 Ron E. Jefferson. All rights reserved.

No part of this book may be reproduced, stored in a retrieval system, or transmitted by any means without the written permission of the author.

Published by AuthorHouse 10/07/2015

ISBN: 978-1-5049-1818-3 (sc)
ISBN: 978-1-5049-1819-0 (e)

Library of Congress Control Number: 2015909973

Print information available on the last page.

Any people depicted in stock imagery provided by Thinkstock are models, and such images are being used for illustrative purposes only.
Certain stock imagery © Thinkstock.

This book is printed on acid-free paper.

Because of the dynamic nature of the Internet, any web addresses or links contained in this book may have changed since publication and may no longer be valid. The views expressed in this work are solely those of the author and do not necessarily reflect the views of the publisher, and the publisher hereby disclaims any responsibility for them.

NKJV

Scripture quotations marked NKJV are taken from the New King James Version. Copyright © 1982 by Thomas Nelson, Inc. Used by permission. All rights reserved.

ACKNOWLEDGMENTS

My deepest appreciation, acknowledgments and gratitude for GOD my FATHER for the INSPIRATION, WISDOM and HIS LOVING presence. Even when I was not aware, or thought. differently.

To my beautiful and loving daugthers JOVAN, PHOENICIA, NINA and KEYANA. You all are my PRECIOUS GIFTS from HEAVEN!

To all my family and friends who encouraged me and knew there was always something GREAT inside me!

To my big brother REGINALD MADDOX for being the FRIEND and INSPIRATIONAL MAN that he has become. And to the memory of my dear mother MARY ALICE JEFFERSON for loving US with everything that she had.

To all my friends VERNITA LOVE, JEANNIE MATTHEWS, RUBY BAILEY and DANIELLE McNEALY at the PINE BLUFF Public Library. For being so hospitable while I composed this entire book in the computer laboratory.

Most of all to my loving, caring, best friend and wife Dr. MARILYN BAILEY-JEFFERSON. Who was given to me to HAVE, HOLD and CHERISH for the rest of our days!

FOREWORD

I could imagine my prince charming long before the rush of adolescence being the one to replace parental authority and become my protector and financial provider; the one who would ask for my hand in marriage and Godly devotion; be my friend, confidant and soul mate; and together we would live happily ever after in a house with a white picket fence. Like so many women, my dreams dissipated into anger and frustration with the realization of that "seemingly unattainable silver lining in life's dark cloud" of relationships, one after the other.

The author, Ron E. Jefferson, offers thought-provoking truths and wisdom to the masses of women scorned and basks in the comfort of male-bashing. He speaks with the hope of bringing unity, understanding, resolution and healthy togetherness to mend relationships suspended in the concomitant milieu of dysequalibrium.

Dr. Marilyn Bailey Jefferson

CONTENTS

FOREWORD

This awesome project was soul-inspired to be a gift to the world of relationships. Many are CHALLENGED, STRUGGLE and FAIL in finding and keeping the one PRAYED for and DREAMED about to be that OH…SO MOST SIGNIFICANT ONE and ONLY.

These written words are intended to ENCOURAGE, ENLIGHTEN and INSPIRE that seemingly unattainable SILVER LINING in LIFE'S DARK CLOUDS.

This opinionated WISDOM I share comes from the masses of LAYMEN that I voluntarily represent! Not to claim ALL KNOWLEDGE with many degrees to give credibility to my thoughts; but I DO have the CONFIDENCE and HUMILITY to believe that there is TRUTH existing without the INSTITUTIONAL background as reinforcement. These TRUTHS come from LIFE EXPERIENCES and are intended to be an adhesive to LIKE THINKING for the sake of UNDERSTANDING, RESOLUTIONS and HEALTHY TOGETHERNESS with the many DYNAMICS that exist between WOMEN and MEN!

My deliberate PRAYER is that EARS will hear for new territory of our HEARTS that will allow new SEEDS to be PLANTED, NURTURED and grow to bear FRUIT that will bless individuals, couples, children, family, friends and strangers that GOD brings into our atmosphere of this LIFE!

'A JOURNEY'

As I walk this path of life, I wonder, "What would GOD have me to do?" Then GOD said, Enjoy this gift I will give you, a day that is brand new!" As I walk this path of life there are times when I feel lonely and often misunderstood. Then I remembered that GOD is always with me and whatever trials I go through HE has prepared them for my good.

As I walk this path of life and there is confusion and I don't know where to go. To the left or to the right. Without taking another step,. I trust GOD completely as the darkness becomes the light.

This path of life can be full of mysteries with so many roads to travel and decisions on which way to turn. It seems that the more I begin to understand. I realize that there is so much more to LEARN!

Ron E. Jefferson ~ Sept. 13, 2002

CHAPTER 1

'BOYS TO MEN'

"MATURE MEN do not STAY the SAME! MATURE MEN are always expecting to ESCALATE and REFINE ourselves! Being BETTER is our GOAL!"

What is the number one ingredient that is so NECESSARY and MISSING at the same time in our MEN TODAY? Excellent question! Well…it is something that comes over a period of time, little by little, at the most unnoticed and seemingly innocent and insignificant of times. It's applied from one soul to another soul, over long and short conversations. It's so POWERFUL and DYNAMIC because of the profound actions that CONFIRM its existence.

It is MATURITY! The great commodity that is laid on a person's HEART and MIND like another coat of fresh paint to redecorate our thinking to EXPAND greater dimensions! It's evident that WISDOM is received and LIVED! WISDOM without application is a SWOLLEN INTELLIGENCE blindly headed toward another DITCH!

When we find ourselves ALL ALONE in our favorite candy store! Mouths watering as we tingle with JOY over GIGANTIC ZOOM-ZOOMS and multi-flavored WHAM-WHAMS! With NO MATURITY we

INDULGE! Then GORGE and stuff ourselves SICK with NO FORESIGHT to understand. Even TOO MUCH of a GOOD thing can and will make us SICK!

Wisdom says EAT some more now, until we are SATISFIED and then come back later, if the opportunity presents itself. Maybe even take a DOGGY-BAG! But once we've made MISTAKES, maturity says "That's enough, remember WHAT HAPPENED LAST TIME!"

Having missed out on the AWESOME experience of having that FRIEND, MENTOR, CONFIDANT person called FATHER, I am thoroughly and totally convinced that the FATHER is the MOST CRUCIAL person and MISSING LINK in the lives of MEN and BOYS today meant to equip us with the GIFT of MATURITY!

Being a LIFETIME card-carrying MOMMA'S BOY, I appreciate every ounce of WISDOM, KNOWLEDGE, SACRIFICE and LOVE that our mothers gave and continue to give with their total UNRESTRAINED COMMITMENT. But it is that MALE-TESTOSTERONE figure that is irreplaceable Their PHYSICAL STATURE, VOICE TONE and VIBE stirs you to FEAR, RESPECT and LOVE just by his merely walking in the room. These MEN are the epitome of what all BOYS and IMMATURE MEN should aspire to be. They are our HEROES and Mt. RUSHMORES that we climb for wealth of KNOWLEDGE and IDENTITY and use to structure our own MALE-DNA. So...WHAT HAPPENED to those ANCHORS that were GOD-given to keep US, our HOMES, NEIGHBORHOODS and SOCIETY from going SHIPWRECK?

In a hyphenated word...SELF-CENTEREDNESS! I believe that is TRUE that a little LEAVEN can and does LEAVEN the WHOLE LUMP! Somehow, some way a SNAKE of EVIL THINKING crept into the gardens of our MALE MINDS and RUINED our HARVEST of REAL MEN! INTEGRITY was given a BAD RAP and labeled with a BAD NAME and obviously left a BAD TASTE in the mouth of many of our PATRIARCHS! SAD, but true! So...what is the SOLUTION to such an IMMENSE PROBLEM and PRESENT SITUATION? Like Rev. Martin Luther King, Jr. said... "Where do we go from here?" We go forward with TRUTH! We MEN of TRUTH stand together side by side and proclaim HONESTY and INTEGRITY in the name of TRUE MANHOOD and re-establish the FRONTLINE! We address these crippling LIES of RESPONSIBILITY HEAD ON! And we dare not FLINCH or RETREAT because our need for MEN in our culture and world is in dire distress and we at an IMPASSE!

"ARE WE THERE YET?"

When we were little boys, we were always wondering "How BIG am I today"? Have I gotten any TALLER since the last time I asked? Which probably, it was YESTERDAY! We would run and go get the nearest CRAYON and find our favorite wall or door trim and turn our backs so that we could mark the wall at the TOP of our HEADS! We were so excited at the SLIGHTEST GROWTH! Even if we have to imagine it! What happened to the desire to GROW UP and be SOMEBODY, to SUCCEED and out do every other little BOY, and be the first one to be a MAN... a REAL MAN? Well the question has to be asked, "How do you know a REAL MAN?" Humph! GOOD QUESTION! Here's a better answer! I was personally BLESSED to grow up in the 60's. I believe GOD placed me in that particular point in time so that I could be a witness to what I know now was the GOLDEN AGE of REAL MEN.

Every TIME has a period and a SEASON! This was a TIME when MEN bonded. They talked endlessly about WHAT REAL MEN DO! They were confirming that AGELESS WISDOM of being a MAN from the generations of REAL MEN before them! We need to understand our roots, where we come from and HOW the HARSHNESS of being a nation that endured, suffered and was ABUSED in every imaginable way as SLAVE DESCENDANTS! Men struggled, endured and encouraged each other side by side to not only survive...but PROSPER in very DARK DAYS.

So what happened to those qualities of BROTHERHOOD that equipped and raised BOYS to MEN? FREEDOM! It seems the irony of freedom has encompassed many minds with personal, family and social AMNESIA! We no longer feel the inner unction that was BRED into boys and men as something, not only necessary, but VITALLY ESSENTIAL.

With the struggle to survive comes COMMITMENT and DEDICATION as part of our upbringing. As wonderful as FREEDOM is, what our forefathers and mothers LIVED, DREAMED, and PRAYED for, we often behave like the SPOILED BRAT child of the wealthy who did nothing more than be born into affluence. It can be taken as a GIVEN, with no sweat from OUR brow in the building of success. It can be assumed by thoughts and behavior that this is the way things ought to be and that everything in the universe is in order.

There must need to be a SLAMMING ON THE BRAKES of this *laissez-faire* mentality that leads to mental SLOTHFULNESS and PHYSICAL IDLENESS. This welfare state of mind has paralyzed many men into the SHADOW of what our FATHER PATRIARCHS...LIVED, BREATHED and DIED with. If we ask any particular group of men today what was the last HARD COVER book they read, after minutes of a BLANK and puzzled look, a vast majority would probably hunch their shoulders as they try to remember the title of that AMERICAN HISTORY book from the 10th grade. Worst yet, they would probably refer to magazines, shrugging with self-delusion about SPORTS Illustrated, TV guide and Play Boy occupying their literary minds. There's an ACHE and longing for those dear brothers of mine to take an HONEST and OBJECTIVE look at their PRESENT lives and FUTURE potential. Before it is too late and OPPORTUNITY has changed to a more viable population group and is not taking any further calls.

Men are born to LEAD, GUIDE and set the MORAL, SPIRITUAL and SOCIAL examples. What happened to the voice that SAYS what they mean and MEANS what they say? If Mr. So-and-So shows up, then everything will work out. It takes a LIFE of educational build up and MUCH processing for this to happen. It won't just happen by praying alone and crossing our fingers, hoping for the best! It takes AFFIRMATIVE and AGGRESSIVE ACTIONS.

"STRENGTH"

The first lesson of BOYS to MEN is STRENGTH, reaching down inside to that ESSENCE of manhood soul, the CORE of who we are and where everything is built on! How so? A man's dominant characteristic is his ability to STAND and WITHSTAND no matter what the opposition, challenge or circumstances. Never GIVE IN! Never QUIT! Never say UNCLE or DIE! This does not rule our common sense. When there is an obvious OVERWHELMING presence...a tactical RETREAT IS THE STRENGTH of WISDOM in those cases!

We are describing the CORE strength of MEN that ultimately exudes through the PHYSICAL, MENTAL and SPIRITUAL fibers of MEN. The challenge for manhood resides in the balancing of his STRENGTH!

Where there is no DISCRETION to appropriately distribute STRENGTH, EGO and pride of STRENGTH can delude reality and be like talking to that BRICK WALL that many sisters complain about. The well balanced man knows his CAPACITIES and ABILITIES! Therein is another dynamic of STRENGTH, Strength of MIND!

MENTAL STRENGTH*

Where the MIND is the BODY will follow. The man's physical BODY, his FAMILY BODY, his Business, Financial, Social and Bodies of opportunities will follow. The man's MENTAL STATE is the first component that is touch by mentorship! Our fathers, uncles, cousins and brothers all cry out in the TENOR voice choir ever since that first RUN and FALL! Get UP! Wipe them tears and GET BACK UP!

They were making a MENTAL BOND and connection. That is the very first thing that we men do! When things get TOUGH, we get TOUGHER! Fear is never ignored! Fear is a HEALTHY human emotion that is given to live with observance and CAUTION, not to be held prisoner by. Not to take hold of the steering wheel of our DAILY DESTINY and leave us stranded on the side of some dark emotional highway, our soul is the furtile ground wherein our GOD created unique person lies. The MIND is the place where seed are sown. The collaboration of MIND and SOULD combines to MOLD and SHAPE each man into his own TRUE SELF.

That MENTAL connection must be NURTURED and maintained. No one FEEDS and CHANGES a baby and then walks away for long periods of time, leaving the infant to CARE for itself. The MIND of a boy is in CEREBRAL INFANCY, thirsty for NEW knowledge like a lost foreign legionnaire dehydrated and delusional from DESERT HEAT.

We men take our young MEN to be under our wings when we are doing repair work on the car and around the home. We break out the TOY TOOL set and let them BANG AWAY on scrap wood or a tire rim. They are thoroughly convinced, even at an innocent age, that WE could not have FIXED whatever was broken without them.

Understanding the DEEP significance of this MEN BUILDING project, we sometimes drag them along when their favorite super heroes are on television; or when their BEST-EST buddy is playing! Shoot! We'll drag little Jamal from down the street because he is in this BROTHERHOOD of MATURITY also. Kicking and screaming they may GO! But we know that dealing with FRUSTRATION and DISAPPOINTMENTS are all a very important part of this MENTAL UPLIFT in ACTION.

Maybe this is why so many FATHERS have abdicated the throne of FATHERHOOD! The daily DEDICATION that some may have mistaken as a GRIND may have been too much for the undisciplined man to CONCEIVE and as a result neglected to FATHER. Not realizing that the SAME effort that goes into the MAN-CHILD will be the same effort that the MAN-TO-BE will provide in our senior years, wheel chairing us around town to the grocery store, doctor and the park to feed the pigeons! Some of us have burned up or retirement plan by not mentoring the ones that will LOVE and care for us in our GOLDEN YEARS!

EMOTIONAL STRENGTH*

This is the area that is so misunderstood, so ONE-SIDED in the minds of BOYS and MEN. The first thing we think of when we consider EMOTIONS is usually related to our FEMALE COUNTERPARTS! This thinking brings any further exploration to a disappointing HALT! Somewhere along the line we have been fed a POISON FRUIT of EMOTIONAL DISCRIMINATION. We have been robbed of that OTHER MALE SIDE; dare I say our FEMININE SIDE! Bam! Some poor brother just SLAMMED this book SHUT or passed out from being PISSED off! Yes my dear brothers, we have a FEMININE SIDE!

Not like 'QUEER EYE' on the STRAIGHT GUY! There is a part of MEN that have that same INTERNAL DNA that is common for HUMAN BEINGS! The GENTLER dynamics within us have been either dismissed as UNMANLY or UNNECCESSARY for the MAN PROJECT!

Many a young man has been LOST within himself, not knowing WHO he fully was inside, me included! The vast amount of young boys is in a dilemma wondering with TENSION and some DARKENING CLOUD of sadness that they may never cross the finish line of TESTOSTERONE! This has proven to be a very EMBARASSING time for adolescent boys to THINK about, with the added pressure of being ostracized for 'GIRLY STUFF'. All we really wanted was some inner understanding! Many women are struggling to this very day with MEN who remained TIGHT LIPPED, only available to give a slightly interested look when conversing due to being emotionally stuck in the eighth grade! Relationships are like taking a Jr. High BOY and sticking him in the local college Pre-Med class and telling him to "WING it...and do the best you can!"

TRUST is major for men! We cannot go AWOL from our well-meaning, but misguided HALF TRUTHS that we got from POOKY and Ray-Ray! If there is going to be growth in MEN and relationships, there has got to be a bridge with a MAN and his EMOTIONAL INNER SELF. Getting permission that it is perfectly legit to CRY, feel lonely, guilty, have a conscience, be considerate and KIND among many other EMOTIONAL SENSATIONS without feeling 'LESS THAN' or a 'SELL OUT'!

SPIRITUAL STRENGTH*

This is the part where the RUBBER meets the ROAD! Why are there so many women in churches that far outnumber the men? Wasn't MAN created before the WOMAN? Why do men FROWN-UP and make the most UGLIEST faces just at the mention of church? If we ASK THE MEN.. about going to church! The first thing they think is SOMEONE DIED! Getting MARRIED! Or go see if they can CHOOSE or get CHOSE! Like CHURCH is the HOOK-UP!

Spirituality runs in the same VEINS AS EMOTIONS! Just on a much higher plane! VIRTUE, MORALITY and SPIRITUAL DISCERNMENT brings a person to himself! A woman's emotions will ventilate and make room for FAITH, SPIRITUALITY and CHURCH! But that MALE PRIDE that was handed down by some UNSPIRITUAL SOUL led many BOYS and MEN down a DARK and SUFFOCATING place called 'EGO'! Many say that EGO means 'EASING GOD OUT! And YES I believe that is so TRUE!

There are parts of our inner person that dwells in elements unseen and unexplainable. The place a where a power greater than ourselves dwell. Where stories of GREATNESS are born and overcoming immense odds for unknown discoveries and VICTORIES reside!

The soul of MAN is the very CORE of who and eventually what he will be! It's the SEED of the soul that lies so deep within! Underneath the layers of HYPE, Identity-Conflict, Identity Discovery, Rumors, Lies,

Misunderstandings, Traditions, Male Ego and Gender preferences lies the person inside waiting for attention, nurturing and development!

This part of the man is where our fore-fathers not only survived. But, THRIVED and SUCCEDED under the harshest and most deprived times of American history. The re was a SOUL BONDING! A reaching out of one man for another man's good and well being. Animosity or comparisons. Just one brother keeping his other brother. Where IRON sharpens IRON!

The understanding and belief that there are MALE limitations are indispensible. MIND, BODY and SPIRIT can only elevate so HIGH and so FAR on it's own! The TRUE realization that there is and must be a GREATER power and being than myself. It's that SOUL pull that longs and cries for bonding of an inner relationship. It's this relationship above all other relationships that build a man into his COMPLETENESS! His WHOLENES

Therein is the anxiety of the core of relationships! If there is no room for a higher belief than a man's own self, then he in essence makes himself his own GOD! The center of his word's attention inevitably revolves... ALWAYS around HIM! His desires! His preferences! All his WANTS and NEEDS!

Many a sister can testify of the resistance and lack of forward momentum in the relationship due to his limited and ONE-SIDED VISION. How else can a man birth children into a world where he willingly chooses to abandon them and not be a part of his own birth right.

Without the knowledge and surrender to a spiritual life. A man is adrift in an ocean of FALSE SECURITY and LIMITED UNDERSTANDING.

Caught up in a tide of PRIDE and headed for the island of ISOLATION, where there are no inhabitants and only BITTER FRUIT to eat!

PHYSICAL STRENGTH*

Here it is! The great PRIDE and JOY of every BOY and MAN! From the time that we're able to RUN, LEAP and PLAY all day. We enjoy the growing strength that we see in FATHER, UNCLE, Big BROTHER and FRIENDS. Our favorite superheroes all had this wonderful gift of GREAT PHYSICAL STRENGTH that we so closely associate with being a MAN!

Like the mighty KING KONG beating on his chest as he stands over another vanquished foe. We beat our chest at an early age to enjoy the sound of the THUMPING that we hear and FEEL! We wake up as little boys and RUN to our favorite wall where we've marked with crayon our last GROWTH CHECK from yesterday. To see how many inches taller we have gotten since the day before. Leaping with JOY at the first sign of increase we would WORK and slowly begin to purpose. Through our frowns. Even if it's in our own imagination!

Our Fathers, Uncles and Male Mentors knew that through the development of our PHYSICAL SELVES they would one day be able to relate our PHYSICAL stature to the deeper male components within us! They would drag us from our favorite cartoon show and stick a rake or broom in our hands to show that our strength has a productive purpose. Through our frowns and grumblings we would WORK and slowly begin to pursue EXCELLENCE in our work. Longing for the approval of FATHER and others who are our REAL LIFE heroes. The ones who first showed us that MEN are to be STRONG!

The message of strength somehow got LOST and MANGLED with its misappropriated use and delinquency. Our strength was given to provide for ourselves, loved ones and those who would come into our world. Never for ABUSE, BULLYING or INTIMIDATION! These are all signs of a BOY or MAN that has a distorted and or perverted sense of MALE IDENTITY.

The privilege and ability to draw satisfaction from a FAIR days labor for a FAIR days pay starts with a RAKE and a BROOM at a young age and grows into the CEO's, engineers, community leaders and dedicated husbands, fathers and men that stand HEAD and SHOULDERS above the rest! They can be seen miles away because they are in a class all their own. The class where REAL MEN BELONG!

'HERE WE GO!'

Now that we have laid down those very informative points for the necessary foundation for what we are about to build in this dialogue. HOLD ON TIGHT! This is where the entire literal conversation get as REAL as REAL goin get!

We are facing desperate times and... beloved, here comes the OVERCOMING MEASURES! Many adages will be referenced and brought to HIGH-DEFINITION life as well as comments, questions and inputs from MALE and FEMALE contributors. After all, I certainly don't want this potential great literary work to go up in the flames of SELF-SERVING BIAS and have detractors accuse me of being MALE NARROW-MINDED.

This is to enlighten both MALE and FEMALE parties about what is and WHAT IS NOT going on in our relationship world. All through the eyes of one of many GOD-LOVING, TRUTH SEEKING and HARDWORKING

MAN that is caught in the CROSS-FIRE of MALE BASHING and MISUNDERSTANDINGS! Not to mention being MISUNDERSTOOD as well!

We will talk about those issues that WOMEN share at the BEAUTY SALON and what we MEN say in the LOCKER ROOM. So by all means… 'LISTEN TO THE MEN' and see, WHAT'S GOING ON? 'What's on our MINDS? And most importantly… WHAT IS THE TRUTH of and about MEN that we haven't OPENED UP about our feelings and deep thoughts about relationships. Well.. LADIES and GENTS, here is what you've been ASKING, WONDERING and probably PRAYING for.

When are the MEN going to SPEAK UP? This is where we SPEAK! And dear hearts… this is only the beginning! So… be CAREFUL what you've PRAYED for! We are PRAYING that you have PRAYED also to be PREPARED for when your PRAYERS will be ANSWERED. And by all means remember that the entire contents of this book is for HEALTH, HEALING and the WHOLENESS of MALES and FEMALES to be wonderfully restored TOGETHER!

CHAPTER 2

'LOVE OR LUST?'

"You know that you have REAL LOVE... when it DON'T STOP!" It's NOT CIRCUMSTANTIAL... like MOODS or the WEATHER! It's always there, never AWOL! And has more to GIVE WHENEVER... NECESSARY!"

HE LOVES ME? HE LOVES ME NOT? SHE LOVES ME? SHE LOVES ME NOT? Those four questions have caused some so much PAIN, DRAMA and RESENTMENTS that many have sworn off relationships all together! Well... at least until their next WARM and FUZZY FEELING kicks in!

What is LOVE? Many are confuse about this question. I would say the MAJOR CONFUSION contributing factor is NOT KNOWING the difference between LOVE and LUST! First of all we need to understand this WONDERFUL and yet so devastating EXUBERANCE know as LUST This PASSION that has the ability to PARALYZE a person to fanatic states! It has destroyed and conquered many a family, nation and a person's LIFETIME REPUTATION.

LUST as defined by WEBSTER'S dictionary as... 'A bodily appetite; especially excessive SEXUAL DESIRE. Overwhelming desire. To feel an INTENSE DESIRE' And from RON's dictionary... 'LUST; The MAD FLESH craving of want, when you want it. And wants it all the time. Regardless of the CONSEQUENCES' Sounds like someone needs a SUPPORT GROUP or THERAPIST! Maybe BOTH!

Is it that our intense DESIRE for LOVE (Or the next closest thang!) we indulge and GRATIFY ourselves to points of PASSION and SEXUAL PLEASURE that we really compromise ourselves in the misguided belief that we are HONING our BEDROOM SKILLS. And getting some HORIZONTAL pleasures to stay VERTICALLY motivated while we deliriously wait on the REAL THANG!

In the mean while living and leaving EMOTIONAL WRECKAGE from mattress to mattress. Living for the weekend with visions of LATE NIGHT and EARLY MORNING escapades dancing in our heads. Without realizing that we are creating a MONSTER within. The more SEX it's fed... the MORE WE WANT!

RED LIGHT! YELLOW LIGHT! GREEN LIGHT!

So are there any signs that we're being PLAYED and MISLED? Surely we won't get any confessions from someone that is satisfied with being our 'FRIEND' with benefits! We need to know from within ourselves... What is LUST in US?

*RED LIGHTS**

Pre-occupation with FASCINATION! Just can't seem to get it off and out of our minds. Here's the funny thang. Women accuse MEN of Sex... SEX... S-E-X! And being a WARM-BLOODIED, PASSIONATE son of a GUN! Heeeeeey... I understand! But come on now! Who made sister TERRY McMILLAN rich many times over with those HOT and STEAMY love novels about SEXUAL INTRIGUE *and* EMOTIONAL SEDUCTION. *Women cultivate their own unique version of* LUST! *All be it a* PINKER *and* SOFTER *version. But ladies it's still* GAS (... *or in the* FEMALE VERSION! LIGHTER FLUID) *that is feeding that* HUNGRY *soul inside for* PHYSICAL *and very* PASSIONATE RELEASE!

GIMME! GIMME! GIMME!

We very quietly and discreetly go about the business of taking care of our personal commitments and daily routines. Always looking over our shoulders and wondering if there just might be some CHINK *in our armor of* PUBLIC PRESENTATION. *Wondering if anyone can possibly smell any of the residual smoke of our* PASSIONATE *soul simmering. We're not bad people! Just with varying degrees from* FLIRTATIONS *to* HORNY *and* NO ONE UNDER 21 *allowed within* HUGGING *distance. We're* FINE *as long as we can get a regular dose of* GIMME... GIMME... GIMME SOME MORE!

We're successful in many areas of LIFE! *Plus... we don't bother* NOBODY! *But there are those times when we want to be* BOTHERED... *or* BOTHER *that someone that's in our sights!* BAM! *There goes that doggone...* GIMME!... GIMME... GIMME ALARM... AGAIN! *Haven't quite found the* RESET *button to just shut it off and then go about our business as usual. Seems like the only* REMEDY *is to just* FEED IT! *Just give it what it wants. The* TOUCH *and being* TOUCHED *by someone. Not just any* OLD SOMEONE! HECK *Naaaaaw! We talking about someone that knows the* HOW! WHEN! *And especially* WHERE *to* TOUCH. *As only* THEY *seem to* KNOW.

Problem is WHERE *is this* MYTHICAL *person? Been going through the usual suspects. At* WORK! DANG! *Been there. Done that! Never again!*

(I THINK! Still living and learning!) CHURCH! *(Forgive US... FATHER!)* The neighborhood *(YIKES! Waaaaay to close for COMFORT!)* Even tried the Fruit and Vegetable sections at our friendly neighborhood grocery store *(Don't do FROZEN!).*

So WOW! Looks like that only leaves US up to our own imaginations! OH BOY! The world is an EXCITING place where ANY and EVERYTHANG GOES! What a reference to go by. Now here we go trying to create our MAKE-BELIEVE world a TRUE REALITY. With the PRINCE and PRINCESS of our version of 'ONE LIFE TO LIVE'!

Everyone we look at potentially a new STAR cast in the episodes of our HOPELESSLY ROMANTIC lives! The SWIRL and RUSH of hearing their lines spoken as we script them into a journey that they have no knowledge of and no awareness! It's in our minds that the WORLD RENOWN director know as 'LUST' dictates line by line and yells 'CUT' and prepares us for another dress rehearsal and more TAKES!

If you find yourself driving by the object of your OUT-OF-BOUNDS PASSIONATE desires house. Just to check and see if they KNOCKING someone else's BOOTS! REDLIGHT!... STOP! No one drives across town just to borrow a cup of SUGAR! ... STOP IT! Calling! Calling! CALLING!... STOP! There are TELEPHONE STALKING LAWS that are being approved state after state every day! SO... STOP IT!

Going to WAL-MART and K-MART wondering if their SKI MASKS will actually help hide your identity when crawling through some bushes trying to get a peek-a-boo in your WANT-A-BE BOO's window! STOP! That's ILLEGAL NOW! These are very extreme cases, but may actually be more and more common than we realize. If you are indulging in these and any similar behavior... STOP NOW! Back away from this book after you place your bookmark and call your local E.A.P. rep and politely explain how much you need to talk to a qualified professional. And then come back and continue reading this LIFE CHANGING book!

YELLOW LIGHT*

This is the mind set of LUST of a lower level. Where there is some moderate control. Not a RAGING 'RED LIGHT' FOREST FIRE. But more like a SIMMERING TEA POT that is whistling with STEAM and HEAT. Ready to be taken off the stove and settle down somewhere COZY and COMFY.

If this were an ADULT MOVIE it would be like SOFT PORN! No CLOSE UP's or EJACULATING SPERM SHOTS! But a more romantic and softer scenario of LOVING and yet with the HEATED PASSIONS. This is the LUST middle ground where a person could BLOW a THERMAL GASKET. Or become like a WARM WINTER BLANKET of LOVING.

I believe this where a majority of MEN and WOMEN are with their SENSOUS selves. The place of INNER ROMANTIC discovery. Where REJECTION and SATISFACTION have a more balanced life span. It's where romantic novels stir the pot of the PLEASURE-filled imagination. Where we grip the wheel of PASSION with a FIRM GRIP. But Not choking the air of anticipation out! Insane SEX FANTASIES are not legitimately pursued as a possible reality. Just the thrill of finding more LOVE than SEX is ever present and motivating.

The CRUCIBLE moments comes when a person has not defined themselves as WHO they are. A LOVER or LUSTER! The YELLOW LIGHT phase of LUST can bend a person either way. All depending on that persons particular SLANT in this delicate, yet HEATED place of SOUL and which course they choose to live on.

As a driver reaches a LIFE INTERSECTION with vehicles of OPPORTUNITY or potential COLLISIONS. The approaching and entering under a traffic signal that has just turned YELLOW will provide little time to make a pertinent decision. Shall I play it CAUTIOUS and not risk SELF INJURY or adventure into the excited yet possible place of WRECKAGE in the search for LOVE!

I would pre-adventure to say that in the YELLOW LIGHT of DESPERATION that many have tested the waters of UNCERTAINTY. Convincing themselves that PRINCE CHARMING or the DREAM GIRL will come to the rescue and save us from ourselves! This being from what I've heard from many has proven to be far more FANTASY than FACTUAL. SLOW DOWN! Look around and observe the other drivers in your life. Avoid the unnecessary SIDE SWIPE of DRIVING BLIND through your LOVE LIFE SEARCHING.

No amount of INSURANCE can guarantee a full recovery from a DRASTIC EMOTIONAL, MENTAL and PHYSICAL abuse or neglect that could have been avoided. Simply by using CAUTION, DISCRETION and PATIENCE. Just like the IMPATIENT TAIL-GATER. It's usually always BEST to let those who demonstrate little or NO CONTROL in areas that you have clearly observed to PASS YOU BY! The YELLOW LIGHT can be a LIFE and EMOTIONAL PERSERVING place if we understand the TRUE RELEVANCE of this very delicate stage of our lives.

GREEN LIGHT*

If LUST CAN BE DEFINED IN THE CATEGORY of a 'GOOD THANG' than here it is! If NOT... Than as the writer and journey teller... I'M

PUTTING IT THERE! LUST is primarily known for its PHYSICAL and SEXUAL attraction! YES! But for the sake of advancing our thoughts beyond what has been established. Let's say that there exist a level of LUST that is not WRECKLESS and UNRESTRAINED.

Let us view a certain amount of LUST at a controllable level; maybe even a place where DESIRE at its HIGHEST level and LUST at its LOWEST level peacefully co-exist and MINGLE!

The GREEN LIGHT is the safe area of human attraction, where CUDDLING is respectfully appreciated! Hand holding, back rubbing and foot massages are the methods of non-verbal communication; a loving look and glance, the unique smile that is shared with NO ONE except the SIGNIFICANT LOVE of your LIFE!

The present beauty THE GREEN LIGHT is that you give yourself permission to "GO"! We have experienced so much of the DARING and DISASTROUS riding through our EMOTIONAL lives with our HEARTS screeching on the brakes of the RED LIGHT mentality and hitting the gas with the PEDAL to the MENTAL running through LUST induced YELLOW LIGHTS!

What a relief to finally find ourselves in the KNOWING of who we are riding comfortably through LIFE under the SAFE SCRUTINY of GREEN LIGHTS! Yes...we are PASSIONATE PEOPLE; though poor judgment and HORMONES has caused us to make UNWISE decisions! We are not BAD PEOPLE! We were just all DRESSED UP and NOWHERE and with NO ONE to COMPLIMENTARY go with!

The people we had attached ourselves to were people with agendas! Looking back we can now see that they were living RED and YELLOW light experiences of their own! So now we live with our SENSES re-claimed and the acknowledgements of SELF-IDENTITY and some relevant SELF DISCLOSURES!

We ride through LIFE with the WISDOM of TAGS, REGISTRATIONS and yes of course the INSURANCE of DIGNITY and SELF-RESPECT to not become NOTCHES on someone else's BED POST! And not MARKING up our own head board... BANGING and getting BANGED through search after search. Behind doors number 1-50 with our fingers crossed hoping that somehow, someway that JUST RIGHT PERSON will fall from the sky like the answered PRAYERS from HEAVEN right into our laps. NO! Not so LOVED ONES! Yes we have learned to trust in our prayers to GOD more than ever!

But we also utilize the GOD-given INTELLIGENCE HE gave us so that we can PRAY MEANINGFULLY and LIVE BETTER.

*MIND OF MEN ~ 'SEX'

So many women wonder is SEX ia all MEN think about? Well... NOT ALL... but YES, QUITE A BIT! WHY? GOD put our desire for PHYSICAL, EMOTIONAL and SPIRITUAL in us to pursue a WIFE! However, once we tasted the GOOD FRUIT of INTIMACY, we departed from GOD'S plan and became OVERWHELMED with SEXUAL PASSION in our own SELFISH PURSUIT! Ever since we stumbled on Uncle Joe's PLAYBOY collection we have been HOT to TROT!

Without GOD maturing us EMOTIONALLY, MENTALLY and SPIRITUALLY in SEXUAL matters we men are swimming in DEEP WATERS! We settle for the AMAZING FEELINGS and not fully embrace the AMAZING WOMEN we engage our bodies with.

We FAIL to mature pass our HIGH SCHOOL mentality of SEXUAL EXCITEMENT. STARING at body parts like an amusement ride at the STATE FAIR. Many treat SEX like a HOBBY or RECREATION and can declare if caught CHEATING... that it didn't mean ANYTHING! Because they just wanted more SEX! DIFFERENT SEX! Just like another MOVIE or VIDEO GAME!

We MEN need GOD! HE uses HIS SPIRIT and WOMEN to bring EMOTIONAL and SPIRITUAL BALANCE to temper our GREAT DESIRE for more, MORE and MORE SEX! It's the MATURE men that wants LOVE and NOT JUST LUST and SEX! Take this to THE BANK!

LOVE*

So FINALLY... What is LOVE? How can we possibly describe such a POTENT word to explain what I believe is not only the GREATEST human emotion. But also the most DYNAMIC LIVING FORCE that there is, was and ever will be!

The dictionary ain't much help. 'LOVE (Noun) The strong affectionate and passion of one person to another person.' Wow! Talk about selling a WORD SHORT. It really all depends on who you ask and what their experience with LOVE is!

GOD bless TINA TURNER for being such a strong, vivacious and talented woman! But there was (and I HOPE it WAS!) for her in life that she believed that LOVE... or LACK of LOVE was something to be forlorned or even scorned with her late hit song 'What's LOVE Got To Do With It?' She sang that song from a wounded heart and abused mind and body.

How many of us have identified with the PAINS associated with LOVE? From the many weeks that song sat at number one on the BILLBOARD CHART. It's obvious that many were in the same boat of UNDERSTANDING. Well, thankfully LOVE does not HURT. And quite frankly, LOVE has everything to do with the RIGHT THANG! It is clear to me and many others that LOVE is being given a 'BAD RAP' and grossly misunderstood by many. Calling it LOVE when in all actuality it is anything but... LOVE!

LOVE chimes! It has it's own distinctly UNIQUE RING to it! Even if it were to be an attempted fabrication. It would be exposed to the LIGHT of TRUTH. Just like holding a SUSPECT $50 dollar bill up to the light for CLEAR and CORRECT AUTHENTICITY. LOVE is ALIVE! It vibrates the MIND, SOUL and of course... the BODY! In heated verbal exchange of PASSION many have pronounced a declaration of LOVE when in fact it was LOVE of what was being done. And not the romantic palpation of the HEART and SOUL in unison with another's HEART and SOUL!

Seemingly the BODY gets in the way of what the MIND needs to hear. It is overwhelmed with the PHYSICAL SENSATIONS that the voice of REALITY and REASON gets drowned out with the MOANS and GROANS of ENDORPHINES GONE WILD!

LOVE is that FRIEND and confidant that instills FIDELITY and FAITHFULNESS! The dictionary stated LOVE as a NOUN. How shallow can a word description be? LOVE is the ACTION WORD that put POWER in the word ACTION! So how does on KNOW if it TRULY is LOVE? The beauty of such an IGNAMIOUS word is it's so evolving that we can't back into a corner and tell it to stay there while we try to figure and find appropriate descriptions.

If you have to ask is it LOVE? Than either it is NOT ! Or the person that is asking does not yet UNDERSTAND how to identify LOVE.

- LOVE SIGNS

First trait of the LOVE DNA is it is given as a PRECIOUS GIFT with the full intention of CARING, NUTURING and being THERE in every imaginable way for another's overall GOOD! It grows when those exact nutrients are returned. Then it is recycled back and forth. Even beyond the GRAVE! YES! I said the GRAVE! LOVE in it's purest form is SPIRITUAL. It is an INVISBLE FORCE that is more FELT than SEEN. However the effectiveness of it is very SEEABLE, TANGIBLE and UNDENIBLE to the most casual observers.

LOVE warms the HEART! Producing such a GLOW that we smile from ear to ear and cheek to cheek at the entrance of our LOVE AFFECTION. There is someone that has TOUCHED, EMBRACED and WATERS our soul with the LIQUID ESSENCE of their own SOUL! There is NO OTHER! LOVE permeates and penetrates all obstacles. What is very much needed and yet unappreciated is the TIME ELEMENT that works in cooperation of LOVE.

What farmer plants seeds and then the next day expects a full grown harvest? LOVE requires NUTURING TIME to PRODUCE. This is where many FAIL to RECOGNIZE and COMMITT to. Anythang worth having is WORTH WAITING FOR! Waiting for LOVE to be revealed and grow is the most valuable personal investment that we will ever incorporate in our human experience.

YES! LOVE is a GIFT! A gift to be highly selective with and shared at various levels and degrees. We don't LOVE everyone the same. But there is LOVE for everyone! Even our enemies. But also, LOVE produces a UNIQUE CHEMISTRY. Where there were TWO PEOPLE with the introduction of LOVE. They begin the LIFE LONG process of 'BECOMING ONE'!

How does this process take place and what are there evident signs to behold?

- TRUTH

The FIRST and foremost sign of all that binds all the other components together is TRUTH! WHO are you? WHO is this person before YOU? This TEDIOUS and sometimes PAINSTAKING adventure tends to BARE ALL over time. The HONEST delivering of those retained and oft times hidden self perspectives provide the observer a WIDER and VERY SIGNIFICANT VIEW. TRUTH allows US to EAGERLY release who we are to this ONE VERY SPECIAL person of our particular importance.

The union is looked upon as SEEMINGLY DIVINE DESTINY. This opens our MINDS and the deep recesses of our OWN ONESS to that particular other person. The vibration and essence of TRUTH and HONESTY that emanates from this person of our affection is like the BAIL BONDSMAN that has the proper resources and wherewithal to help FREE US from ourselves. To OPEN up those tightly kept corners of our identity where previously 'NO ONE WAS ALLOWED'!

TRUTH flows through the veins and very fibers of the soul of it's carriers. We sense it! We feel and VIBRATE IN and right along with it. It is the SOUL REFRESHING SHOWER that bathes us in a pure downpour of 'FREE RELEASE'! Where there is the sense of LACK OF TRUTH is a TREMNDOUS 'RED FLAG' that cannot and should never be DISMISSED or IGNORED!I am personally always amazed at how women who are born, gifted and created with GREAT INNER INTUITION. To only drown out those inner voices screaming at the top of their lungs only to settle for a FLING, ONE NIGHT STAND or a COMPROMISING relationship instead.

TRUTH should stand at the gate of our emotions and search for TRUE VALIDITY before they can safely pass into our conscious minds. We should FRISK those contradictory feelings over a period of TIME... TIME... TIME! How many times have we rushed off HEAD LONG into emotional and potentially dramatic situations HALF-COCKED and OVER-LOADED. With VOLITALE SENSATIONS that wound up doing more DAMGE and HARM than GOOD. The necessary damage control cost more in EMOTIONAL RE-COOPERATION and possible FINANCES than the original issue itself. When will we learn that our FEELINGS and EMOTIONS are meant to SERVE US as references and not as VIGILANTES. They are given to CONFIRM that there is something GOOD to be maintained or something BAD that needs to be addressed or ERADICATED.

How much DENIAL of TRUTH and the resulting PAIN it brings are we willing to endure before we seek SOLUTIONS and NECESSARY CHANGE. Somehow and for some strange reason... we allow our EMOTIONS to DICTATE and HARNESS us to unhealthy illusions and fantasies of ‘MAYBE THIS’ and ‘MAYBE THAT’ or ‘ONE DAY’. Only to hear the repeated voice of TRUTH say... WHY?... WHY?... WHY? When it’s clear voice was that beacon of light from the lighthouse of SAFE SAILING saying... ‘COME THIS WAY’! Follow me into SAFE HARBOR.

TRUTH! The undeniable GLUE that HOLDS, BUILDS and BINDS all relationships for a BEAUTIFUL NOW... and LOVELY FUTURE.

Without TRUTH we are DOOMED to crash into the harsh tragedies of the LIES of DANGEROUS CORAL REEFS of DESPAIR and GREAT DISAPPOINTMENT. And possibly a long time of independence from SELF-HUMILIATION. TRUTH always HEALS and DELIVERS!

- "What are you LOOKING at... when you LOOKING for LOVE?"

*TRANSPARENCY

What are you using when you're looking for LOVE? Certainly not LOOKING in the WRONG places anymore! I'm praying that you're NOT! And definitely PRAYING for you if you are! But even in the SO-CALLED RIGHT places. What are you using to look with? And what exactly are you looking for?

Well... obviously we use our eyes. That's the first line of SCURTINY. With so many BROKEN-HEARTED women and MEN (YES! I said BROKEN-HEARTED MEN!) HURT probably DEEPER Men do get damaged in failed relationships far more than known, acknowledged or even talked about. But we're going to talk ALL ABOUT IT! Men have a tendency to submerge their feelings of hurt probably DEEPER than they ever have before.

Women may cover pain with CHURCH, LOVE NOVELS or another declaration of PART-TIME, LIFE LONG CELIBACY rather than seek the essential HEALING Men may drown their sorrows in a 12-pack of BUD LITE or HENNESY by the liter. Then with many GRUNTS and GROANS we pull all-nighters watching ESPN. Eventually.. some drift out to PAYBACK the nearest female victim with some GOOD 'OL... WHAM-BAM... Thank you Ma'am sexcapade.

These PAIN-FILLED emotions dwell deep and reside on our INSIDE, then wee better fitted when we can employ a DEEP INNER VISION. I'm confident that there are many reading this literary piece right now that can attest to how a GOOD LOOKING and SEXUALLY attractive person may not possess the compatible chemistry for REAL LOVE.

So here we are. Those goose bump feelings that have us TINGLING at the very thought of our newest LOVE INTEREST in our cross-hairs. We know we like what we see! But... I remember our momma's saying... "Everythang that may look GOOD to YOU...!" Yeah... you already know the rest!" We look long enough and DEEP enough to where we can sense more than what we SEE! Now... somehow we begin to see them in NEW and DIFFERENT light. Their TONE! Facial expressions! Body language! And even what they DON'T SAY... begins to speak to us! On our INSIDE! Problem is we move to SWIFTLY! IMPATIENCE is still the number ONE CULPRIT when it comes to sliding down the slippery slope of ANOTHER ONE BITES THE DUST relationship.

We jump into our EMOTIONS and convince ourselves that TIME is irrelevant, We can see ourselves one day walking down the aisle of MATRIMONY and don't even know enough about them to fill up an INDEX CARD! Let what you SEE collaborate with what you SENSE and FEEL over a period of TIME! This keeps our EMOTIONS from distorting WHAT we SEE! And even more important... WHAT WE THINK WE SEE!

You will begin to sense a 'TUGGING' or a 'PULLING' of your MIND and SPIRIT that will guide you if you let them into what to do next. It may be small seemingly insignificant steps. But these small inclinations will lead to the next BEST maneuver which sheds MORE LIGHT! This will give a sense of X-RAY VISION! Which gives more CLARITY! Ask a friend about some RELATIONSHIP SCENARIOS. Don't claims these episodes being about YOU. This will help to keep them NEUTRAL and UNBIASED. Than SEE and SENSE what they SEE! Nothing like having GOD-SENT FRIENDS to run some REAL-LIFE situations by.

Their ability to discern is given to them to ASSIST YOU! Just like your ability to discern is given to HELP THEM as well as YOURSELF. The great and uncontested value of having FRIENDS! Their gifts are PRECIOUS for each of us to use what you see with your INNER VISION will either place them in the LIGHT of TRUTH or the SHADOW of UNCERTAINTY.

Do you continue to drive down roads that are UNMARKED with UNCLEAR VISION ahead? I certainly PRAY NOT! Yet some choose to RATIONALIZE this quasi PRINCE CHARMING and BELL OF THE BALL want-to-be into someone they can creatively FIT and CHANGE into that just RIGHT person. Can you spell D-I-S-A-S-T-E-R? Brake out the CRYING TOWELSNOW! We have a better chance of CHANGING OURSELVES than the people around us that we choose to LIKE, ADMIRE and maybe LOVE. Yet some still try ! In VAIN.... Because they LEAPED... when they should have LOOKED! And LOOKED well!

*NUTURING

Here is LOVE at it's most SENSITIVE BEST! That TANGIBLE and one of the most prominent descriptions of LOVE ... UNDENIED! That intimate and NON-SEXUAL CARING for ONE ANOTHER. The driving and motivating energy is the SUPREME well being for and of your partner. There is a sense of SACRIFICE that doesn't even feel SACRIFICIAL. It's as if what I'm doing for you and your GOOD is somehow and in some inexplicable way makes ME better!

This is that SPIRITUAL BINDING and BONDING taking place. That's where me and those who would purpose a 'LOVE AT FIRST SIGHT' encounter would DIFFER! LOVE is ACTION as much and in many cases more than our WARM and FUZZY EMOTIONS. Who wants to get out of a comfortable bed at UNGODLY hours of the night. Then stand in a long WAL-MART line with 30 sleepy and grumpy people with only three over-worked and GRUMPY CASHIERS. To get some ALMOND PECAN CLUSTER SWIRL ice cream with a bag of HO-HO's? Only those of us who CARE so much for our LOVED ONE that we GRUMBLE a little out the door. Only to STOP and be thankful for that AWESOME person that is a GIFT who would do the same and much more for US! Yeah... WOW!

Nurturing is so vast that it covers many bases. Not just medicinal type. But the ACKNOWLEDGING TYPE also. Wee the exclusive outlet when they need to talk and tell. Sometimes even RATTLING ON and ON. Well that time of listening is very therapeutic for the one speaking. And surprisingly for the LISTENER as well. We have long days and many challenges from day to day. It's that patient LOVE that will allow us to unfold and unravel. We twist and UNTWIST our way out of CONFUSION and DRAMA from job, family and sometimes our own thinking!

There is the this EVER-PRESENT ROMANTIC NURTURING! As a healthy and very PASSIONATE man I must divulge that there are a group of men that enjoy the interludes before the main events of life. AFFECTIONATELY SPEAKING! The MATURE MAN becomes more and more a SENSITIVE BEING like the woman already is from her own FEMININE DNA.

WE want the SOFT TOUCHES! The WORDLESS conversations of our VIBRATIONS mingling together in our own PRIVATE ATOMOSPHERE. We journey in a world where we make LOVE apart from our PHYSICAL NATURE and LOVE each other in the MIND, HEART and SOUL! These are the LOVE TREMORS before the actual PASSIONS of VOLCANIC ERUPTIONS!

*CHEMISTRY

LOVE BINDS! LOVE BUILDS! LOVE is the ULTIMATE ADHESIVE that can extend beyond the GRAVE! We can sit somewhere off to our own selves and reminisce at the recollections of the WARM EMBRACE and SOFT KISSES of our love one. And their presence is so REAL it's as if they are just away on a BUSINESS TRIP even when they have gone on to ETERNITY ahead of US!

There is a UNIQUE chemistry that is created when LOVE is present. It brings TWO distinct MINDS and PERSONALITIES into an arena of SAME-LIKENESS and UNION unlike any other! Our individual personalities come together to create a BLENDED PERSONA that does not and never have existed before this UNION of LOVE. It is a catching up of the souls whirling around in their own venue to explore and delve deeper into one another.

Yes... RARE! I guess you could say! But I would reply to look closely at the BLESSED ONES who have discovered this PURE BONDING. They brought their committed chemistry of MIND-SET, MORALITY and SPIRITUAL principles into their CORE IDENTITY!

1. NON-COMPROMISING! Ask me if I would like to drive this 1987 FORD PINTO just t get around in and maybe even save a little MONEY. And put some PATIENCE into practice and with

that SAVED MONEY and in due time be the proud owner of an UPGRADE of your AFFORDABLE CHOICE! We make the necessary SACRIFICES to avoid making COMPROMISES and SETTLING for LESS! If we can remain PATIENT!

2. POSITIVE SELF-KNOWLEDGE! Knowing who you are will keep you on your road to your DESTINY! Not allowing current FRUSTRATIONS or past DISAPPOINTMENTS festering and infecting our HEALTHY SELF-IMAGE. That we have fought long and hard to build and maintain. It's the POSITIVE image of ourselves that we see daily that confirms our own estimation of our value and worth.

   Depending too much on the opinions of others estimations has paralyzed and stymied far too many into a FALSE and NEGATIVE self-image of themselves! Stay positive with a diet of HEALTHY THINKING. Read what promotes and not DEMOTES! Negativity has a SNEAKY way of creeping in uninvited through mental doors that we unintentionally leave ajar.

3. COMPASSION BREEDS PASSION. This is where we debunk the thought of 'NICE GUYS' finish last. It's a wicked deception to make many to believe that KINDNESS is weakness. WISDOM must accompany our KINDNESS! When we lack discretion we allow misuse and manipulation an opportunity to run roughshod over us. Like energetic children at recess on their PLAYGROUND. KINDNESS is a GREAT VIRTUE that is much needed in our world today. The people who propose this ill idea are those who are either MEAN-SPIRITED and need our HELP more than most. Or they were deceived

and transformed themselves from the NICE people they were into COLD-HARDED cases in need of a BAIL BOND! BE NICE! BE KIND! It is the lubricant that keeps our world from CORRODING into a scrap heap of emotionless ZOMBIES that feed off of each other instead of LOVING each other.

Whether there is someone SPECIAL to LOVE in CLOSE PROXIMITY or if it's doing acts of KINDNESS to whomever crosses our life's pathway. The KINDNESS that we display is released into the environment of our LIVING SOULS! Touching people in ways that are SPIRITUAL. Where our vibrations of GOOD and EQUITY penetrate the HARDEST of HEARTS and where MEANESS is turned into FREEDOM!

*FRIENDSHIP

LOVE creates many plateus for individuals and couples to reside and dwell in. I would dare say that LOVE begins in FRIENDSHIP, Friendship is the place where ATTRACTION has been confirmed. It is that origin of SPIRITS blending. It is a level of LOVE that has innocent beginnings and can culminate in a LIFELONG adventure in ROMANCE and HARMONY through the profoundness of FRIENDSHIP.

When we discover LOVE, FRIENDSHIP is not dismissed to the back of the room like an UNWANTED OLD TOY! Friendship continues to THRIVE! That is, if FRIENDSHIP ... like LOVE is being NURTURED. For instance, ever NOT quite LIKE someone YOU LOVE at a given moment? And yet you wouldn't THINK for a MOMENT of DENYING the LOVE you have for that SAME PERSON! Well.. the same could be said for someone where LOVE was vacated ... BUT! Lo and behold there is a LIKING that trails after them like the local HOUND chasing after the MEAT TRUCK!

LOVE continues to FLAME the FRIENDSHIP that started this CHEMISTRY. We always have FRIENDSHIP to FALL BACK on and at the same time re-enforce the ROMANTIC COMMITMENTS. That is what makes BREAK-UPS so devastating. The BETRAYAL of LOVE and the DENIAL of FRIENDSHIP. These are links that provide the stability that AFFAIRS, FLINGS and ONE-NIGHT stands just don't have. Those are built on SELF-CENTERED GRATIFICATION. While FRIENDSHIP rides LOVE giving direction for SAFE PASSAGE and always on the SURVIVAL LOOK-OUT!

There is a blending of these AFFECTIONATE components as well as between the LOVE BIRDS. Friendship blends so CLOSELY and so well with LOVE that LOVE and FRIENDSHIP experiences the same ONESS that the TWO in LOVE experience. There becomes so SLIGHT a difference it is virtually unnoticeable Friendship becomes a REFERENCE POINT as well as a CORNERSTONE within a relationship. How else can two people spend multiple years together in an ENTHUSIASTIC and VIBRANT STATE? Friendship gives birth to a COMPANIONSHIP which makes way for those components of relations to compose themselves into the adhesiveness of the 'ONENESS PROCESS'.

I believe that many become pre-maturely disenchanted over the thoughts of LIFETIME relationship because they have drawn a line of 'OBSOLETENESS' to relationships. As is to say that it's become a commitment of EXISTENCE rather than EXCITEMENT! Years of being together are intended to BUILD TOGETHER. Not just some DREARY TOLERATION of EXISTENCE together.

Friendship thrives on ongoing discovery and activity together. When there is NO RELATING with each other in proven ways of POSITIVITY together. The relationship deadens as sure as a FLOWER in the corner SHUT OFF from the warmth of the SUN and very little... (if any) WATER!

*COMMUNICATION

Women TALK! MEN don't TALK! That's the PERCEPTION for many and TRUTH in many ways. Why don't MEN TALKJ is the DEEPER question? And why do WOMEN TALK SO MUCH? Is another if not a better question! Well... Can we just go back to MALE/FEMALE DNA? If nothing more than GOD'S design, women are more VOCALLY pre-disposed. MEN can TALK, but have reasons they/we choose not to. (Hold that THOGUHT!) But please don't make the mistake of thinking or believing that WE are NOT LSITENING. A man is LISTENING... even if he is ACTING LIKE he isn't! He has probably already EMOTIONALLY moved out. He's probably the committed type of habitual convenience and behavior/ And AIN'T GOING NOWHERE... or making plans to! MAYBE SOON!

COMMUNICATION is evidence of CARE and CONCERN. Even for the tightest-jawed men. Words must be SPOKEN at some TIME and POINT. Conversations can HELP or HURT anyone. MEN so because a woman's words will either BRING HIM OUT or PUSH HIM BACK further into his CLAMSHELL.

Women are so EMOTIONALLY WIRED that what they say some MEN may consider inconsequential. Accusing them of letting there EMOTIONS doing their TALKING for them. A woman will take those CAPTIVATING words and will resound them over and over in her head! Sleep and AWOKE! Yes!... Yes!... Yes! Actions SPEAKER LOUDER than WORDS! But WORDS do SPEAK and can be LOUD as well. But like Grandmamma said... 'The PROOF is in the PUDDIN!' It's there to taste for yourself! But words can MOVE and REMOVE a person EMOTIONALLY speaking.

There's NO greater JOY than to see the person of your LOVE interest light up when YOU SAY... WHAT YOU SAY! It being those GOOD, HEALTHY and NURTURING words that continue to BUILD and BIND the TWO into ONE. Consequently... our HEARTBREAKS have come from FIERY words pf ANGER and BELITTLEMENT from someone that promised us NOTHING but LOVE FOR US!

Men without confidence in themselves and their HIGHLY-SECURED EMOTIONAL position will withdraw and avoid conversations that they feel will only confirm their disturbance... if not OUTRIGHT FEARS! Though HIDDEN deep under our veil of VIRAL MASCULINITY. There is that foreboding NEVER-ENDING, DRAWN-OUT conversation that many men wish they had never brought up or been or been available to. Many women are more well versed in COMMUNICATION and YIELD it like a surgeon does a SCAPEL. And many MEN fear with the ANESTHESA of COMPLIANCE... we would NOT COME OUT the SAME

So we must talk to each other. No one (Not even you GIFTED sisters!) can READ MINDS! No matter how much some MEN fear you can! WORDS must be placed into our relationship atmosphere. Either for EMBRACEMENT or REJECTION. This is always better than wading around in the FOG of UNCERTAINTY. Many women claim they want to KNOW what men are thinking! My humble advice is to be PREPARED for what you may not WANT or EXPECT to hear.

Maybe better to get some indication by INDIRECT means! Piece meal style. A little bit here and a little bit there. That would give you more preparation time as well as some SLANT on his thinking. And will provide him with a SAFE passage for verbalizing himself in a NON-THREATENING environment. COMMUNICATION is a KEY that will unlock FEAR, DOUBT and WORRY. And will build TRUST, CONFIDENCE and PEACE for LOVE to find out where and HOW each one is doing.

*SACRIFICE

LOVE entices the HIGHEST GOOD for the other. Even to the restraining of one's own self and personal desires. This is when and where the relationship becomes LAYERED TOGETHER. The fibers being where each one fulfills the others WANTS and NEEDS. There is a very ironic thing about this phase of relationship for those that do HOLD OUT! Setting a little aside for themselves at the expense of WIDENING the BORDERS of the US to grow and expand. Actually restrains the DYNAMIC EXPANSION of what... SHOULD HAVE BEEN!

When there is a person in your life that is LOVING, AFFECTIONATE, CARING and NURTURING with KNIDNESS and undergirded with deep levels of FRIENDSHIP. What is done in SACRIFICE becomes a PLEASURE. It is the SURETY that LOVE flows from one another. In some COSMIC way when LOVE is the overriding motive. What is done for ONE is actually having the same equivalent effect and result of doing for YOURSELF! To someone on the outside looking in... they may not have the INTIMATE perspective or vision to see the depth of where LOVE flows through these BLESSED ONES. There is an old saying... 'IF YOU LIKE IT! I LOVE IT!"

The mutual respect that they have for each other will not allow them to take advantage of or misuse the other. The ONENESS process that has encompassed them is unilateral. Their JOY is your JOY! Their PAIN ... is your PAIN! There is more TOGETHERNESS evolving and LESS and LESS SEPARATIONS.

SACRIFICE say's... "Even though I may WANT something. My growing and even greater desire is that I WANT you to have SOMETHING... MORE!" Then you have two individuals that care more about the other as much as themselves. Neither one will go LACKING! What YOU have is MINE! What I have is YOURS is the motto they live by! And where SCARIFICE has a new face and takes on a new meaning when there is LOVE. SACRIFICING for the one you LOVE has supernaturally become a JOY! Because you know that many LOVE OFFERINGS of SACRIFICE are yours to COME!

*FAITHFULNESS

The ultimate component of tangible LOVE is what many CRY OUT for at times and DOUBT the existence of and PRAY for is... FAITHFULNESS! Here lays the GRAND PUBA of what LOVE has to do with IT Can individuals who have grown together in many ways remain TRUE to the other? It will definitely take the whole being of a person, which is MIND, BODY and SOUL!

MIND – The indwelling thought life of where we and GOD alone domains. Those secret thoughts and fantasies are played out like actors on a stage. Someone has provocatively stated that the MIND is a battlefield. Well... with that being TRUE. We must arm ourselves from OURSELVES as well as others. The sensual side of who we are and who we are committed to MUST be protected like a 'BABE' in the woods. We dare not allow ourselves to be put into situations that would compromise our INTEGRITY of FAITHFULNESS. We may need the aid of a TRUSTED family member, friend or mentor to release any divisive thoughts that would cause us to SKID off the road of the HONORABLE into the DITCH of DISLOYALTY.

We must build a MENTAL FORTRESS and MENTAL FORTITUDE to keep our COMMITMENT to FAITHFULNESS in order. We indulge in a MENTAL DIET of POSITIVITY and OPENNESS to allow TRANSPARENCY to work on us and within us. It's when we step into the MENTAL SHADOWS of SECRECY that we lose our way and forget who are the most IMPORTANT people in our lives and the PRECIOUS place that they and they ALONE HAVE!

BODY – Ever heard the saying... 'The MIND is WILLING! But the BODY is WEAK!' Yeah... well that was a MAN that said that! As a matter of FACT. If the TRUTH be told... WE men would admit that is our NATIONAL THEME SONG! (We are going into much GREATER DETAILS in the next chapter! So don't change the channel!)

My BODY! My BODY! Just echoes across the PLANETARIUM of our mental landscape. OVER and OVER this body of FLESH craves ATTENTION! WHY?.... You ASK? For S-A-T-I-S-F-A-C-T-I-O-N on so many FRONTS. But our greatest and most formidable attention getter is SEXUAL by PURE NATURE.

How many songs have been crooned by gifted singers bemoaning their aching loins bulging to the point of near UNBEARABLE INSANITY! Any form of RELAESE with whomever is willing and unfortunately... UNWILLING VICTIMS there may be ... WILL DO! If our minds are the catalyst for ACTIONS and LIFE STYLES, then our BODIES must fall in line. Like the dedicated soldier following HIGH RANKING orders from the REGIMENT COMMANDER. We must submit our bodies to follow an almost PRE-ORDAINED way of being. This is a sign of the GREAT MALE MATURITY that is absentee in so many MEN.

The solution is easier understood than it's PERPLEXING APPLICATION. Why launch out into the DEEP when you have never graduated from the WADE POOL! Even OLYMPIC SWIMMERS train for their AQUATIC endeavors. So we must pay ATTENTION to our own EROTIC GAUGES. And not let our SENSUAL SIDE maroon us into those SHARK infested waters without a LIFE PRESERVER!

Don't go to an ATM at night for a QUICK WITHDRAWAL! Don't keep letting your eyes linger on the LIPS, HIPS, THIGHS and CLEVAGES that creates AROUSAL like FOREST FIRES. Some thangs just have to become a PRECIS CODE of CONDUCT on our PHYSICAL level of living that will help sustain Us... from US!

SPIRIT – Someone many suns and moons ago said... 'GOD will DO for US what we CANNOT DO for OURSELVES!' This is the principle and power of developing and nurturing our SPIRITUAL... INNER SELVES. What the MIND and BODY needs in such a COMPREHENSIVE way is the third BINDING CONNECTION of our spirit. Like the GOVERNMENT structure of PRESIDENT, SENATE and CONGRESS. The MIND, BODY and SPIRIT work together to compose the overall BEST and GOOD opportunities and outcomes.

The spiritual MIND has it's greatest resource through the relationship with the ALMIGHTY SPIRIT, which is GOD! We have lost our way when we exclude the SPIRITUAL MIND from our temporal decisions.

Appealing to our INNER SELVES helps remove the STRONG ILLUSIONS that our bodies crave and our mind creates. This is the STRUGGLE many MEN will not discuss and further more are not even aware of this GREAT INTENSE DILEMMA! I say this because many MEN are so prone to just GIVE in to this DESIROUS SWAY that no INNER CONVICTION or CONVERSATION ever evolves.

Then when the act of COPULATION is done and the SMOKE clears. Many will be in complete dismay at the DAMAGING circumstances around them, proclaiming... 'What have I done?' This is where SPIRITUAL MENTORING! Men of FAITH! Religious affiliations will nourish the SEED of our spirits and will bloom into a man guided by PRINCIPLES and not by his LOWER PELVIC REGIONS!

*MIND OF MEN ~ 'LOVE!'

For us MEN, we demonstrate LOVE by our actions. We DEDICATE OURSELVES to GOD to LEAD and GUIDE US. As real men of FAITH, MORAL and INTEGRITY. We cook breakfast in BED! We WINE and DINE! We understand the difference between SEX and LOVE!

We enjoy the feelings of just a NICE HUG and want plenty of THEM! We protect from HURT, HARM, DANGER and RUDENESS! We FIX those thangs... that are BROKEN. But we often need help VERBALIZING our feelings of LOVE!

We don't SMOTHER or SUFFOCATE with SUSPISCION. We FATHER and shower our children with LOVE and AFFECTION! We don't let OUTSIDERS in and cause DISTURBANCES. We live to PLEASE and LOVE the sound of HAPPY VOICES and BIG PRETTY SMILES! WE GIVE EVERYTHANG we GOT and ONLY ask for EVERYTHANG you have be GIVEN BACK... to US!

CHAPTER 3

'CHEATS, LIES, STEALS!'

"Better to be ROBBED with a KNIFE or GUN than by an.... IMAGINARY RELATIONSHIP!"

It seems like ALL the GOOD MEN are TAKEN!!! Bemoans many single and ELIGIBLE women who are so fed up with 'NO GOOD CHEATING MEN!' We all have heard about the disproportionate number of WOMEN to MEN. To whom very many men ROAR a BIG YELL of approval across the land! Why? Because with those OUT-OF-WHACK numbers... brothers can be very CHOOSEY! Even brothers that don't quite have it all together can get a HOOK-UP! Some very TOGETHER women may COMPROMISE and settle down for a MALE PROJECT that she can MEND and FIX into a REAL GOOD BROTHER... ONE DAY! (Maybe!)

But the number one EPIDEMIC PAIN of the WOMEN NATION are the BUMPS and BRUISES they have incurred from their search for PRINCE CHARMING! Or at least like ARETHA FRANKLIN said... 'A MR. DO RIGHT MAN!' CHEATING is defined as to SWINDLE or FRAUD. To FOIL, DEPRIVE or ELUDE. To be SEXUALLY UNFAITHFUL... OFTEN. In our days of WOMEN'S LIBERATION and EQUAL RIGHTS. Many women have taken on the HARD-CORE MANTRA of MEN where SEX is SOCIALLY ACCEPTABLE ACTIVITY between CONSENTING adults where all is FAIR on the MORNING AFTER! NO HOLDS BARRED... KNOCK DOWN! DRAG OUT! Every MAN or WOMAN for themselves style of DATING! So some statistics (Depends on the source and WHO you're asking!) will confide that there is a RISE in the area of INFIDELITY among women.

This is the part of the book where my friends and associates chime in with their QUESTIONS and COMMENTS. After all... I don't want you all to THINK that all this book is just about my THOUGHTS and OPINIONS.

- BERNADETTE C. (GA.) ~ "Why is it so HARD for MEN to STAY COMMITTED?"

WHY... Oh WHY is it so DIRE that many MEN struggle to be and STAY FAITHFUL? Especially when the relationship is GOOD and with a GOOD WOMAN! Just NO REAL EXCUSE or REASON for MEN to NOT KEEP IT ZIPPED and LOCKED UP for the person that they are committed to. Well... this is the REAL GROWN-UP, JUICY part of the book where the REAL TALK is about to be DROPPED... because (YES!) it is HOT!

- Do you REALLY, REALLY want to know WHY MEN CHEAT?... REALLY?!... OK!

First of all, MEN CHHEAT because THEY CAN! Hey!... Hey! CALM DOWN! Fix ya FACE! We talking ACCOUNTABILITY! RIGHT?... OK! Mr. SMOOTH ain't out there CHEATING by HIMSELF! He doing it with someone else. Now albeit he may be deceiving some poor FATHER'S DAUGHTER. But my delicate contention with all you BEAUTIFUL,

GOD-blessed woman is… "IF YOU KEEP DOING WHAT YOU DOING! YOU GOING TO KEEP GETTING WHAT YOU BEEN GETTING!

- What CHEATERS Do!

STOP trying to SEX men into RELATIONSHIPS and MARRIAGE! You can have his BABY if YOU WANT TO! And if HE turns out to be a 'NO GOOD CHEAT' What in the name of the 'FRONT DOOR' makes you think… all of a sudden when little SHANIQUA or JAMAAL get here that he going to turn into a FAITHFUL MATE and FATHER. That's the UNHEALTHY, ROMANTICALLY TWISTED thinking that has left many women as single parent mothers STRUGGLING and MAD at the WORLD! When they could have made WISER decisions without their HORMONE driven desires and EMOTIONS and been HEALTHIER WOMEN TODAY! MORAL: 'Keep ya LEGS CLOSED and ya MIND STRAIGHT!

Now back to the CHEATERS! Granny and Momma was RIGHT! WAIT!... WAIT!... WAIT! If it's just SEX he wants… HE AIN'T GOIN WAIT too LONG! Protecting your HEART from being ABUSED and USED and MISUSED as a SEXUAL PLAYTHANG is what's MOST IMPORTANT! All that RUBBING and TOUCHING! Why HE always so CLOSE. Almost SITTING on your LAP! BREATHING HARD! Licking them BIG LIPS. How many times did you catch him staring you… UP and DOWN! MERCY!... MERCY ME!

Please pay ATTENTION to someone's RESTLESSNESS. They are anxiously trying to make contact. Like a BATTER waiting on that JUST RIGHT PITCH. Something that he's confident that he can get a 'GOOD HIT'. Then you better believe once they are safely on base. They are trying HARD to get to SECOND BASE… even if they have to STEAL! (We will go into EMOTIONAL THEIVERY later!) Can you not sense that ANXIOUSNESS beneath all that well cropped CALM?

The plan is to move from one place of COMFORT to the next designated space to recline into your NAIVETY. When engaging someone in the affairs of the HEART. The EMOTIONAL GAURDS should be let down S-L-O-W-L-Y! Even METHODICALLY after there has been tangible and distinguishable PROOF of... WHO THIS PERSON IS! And not whom he THEATRICALLY presents himself to be. While the focus of these points are primarily directed at MALE composites. These signals are universal in the regard of gender. These apply to everyone in general. I'm bringing clear descriptions for the INTELLIGENT woman who have yet to delve deeper into the MALE MENTALITY. And are wandering in levels of a 'LITTLE GIRL LOST' references.

- WHAT CHEATERS SAY?

I can recall my 6th grade recess in the gymnasium where there were FUN and GAMES galore. Some were playing BASKETBALL, HOP-SCOTCH and all different BOARD GAMES. But at this one particular table there was a young boy and girl. He was kind of CURLED UP to her at their own private table. He was so COOL! Relaxed. Seemed like he had a conversation that was very much under HIS CONTROL!

He had that little girl just BEAMING and GLOWING with laughter! I turned my attention to my other friends and classmates. But every so often I would hear that same little girl burst into another fit of HUMOROUS BLISS! Wow! What in the world is HE SAYING to HER? He seems to have her completely nailed to her seat and TOTALLY... CAPTIVATED!

Not fully aware of the significance here of this youthful interplay at my early age. But there was the THOUGHT of a SEED being PLANTED. My wondering what in the SUSAN B. ANTHONY dollar coin was he saying! This stayed with me to be understood later in LIFE. That was a CLEAR DEMONSTRATION of the POWER of WORDS.

*So... What DO YOU DO when you hear something that is ALMOST to MUCH (... yet BEAUTIFUL... and MUSIC to the EARS!) to BELIEVE?

I would venture to say that the SWOONING does just what it was and is intended to DO! Dull the LOGIC, STABILITY and SENSIBILITY of COMMON SENSE and eventually MORALITIES. Where the EMOTIONS are being manipulated and can be used against YOU! Women are so known for wanting to get the FACTS. Building an IDENTITY PROFILE. GOOD! But when someone has a CHEATER mentality they are STUDYING YOU more advantageously and precisely more than you are THEM. While you are listening for certain answers. They are studying your TONE, FACIAL and BODY expressions. Your SLIPS of the LIPS! Your pauses! And they tend to anticipate where you are going with your CONVERSATIONS before you even go there!

The CHEATER is a FOX! Sniffing on your mental and EMOTIONAL trails to see how WARM it is to measure how close he is to being CORRECT in his DEVIOUS NAVIGATIONS.

- How to discern the MELODIOUS and SWEET TONE of DECEPTION!

Have you ever heard them APOLOGIZE? Admit a WEAKNESS? STUTTER? These words of an INSINDERE SOUL are very well rehearsed. They don't know that they can be detected without their AWARENESS. Now... I'm certainly NOT trying to feed

UNWARRANTED INSECURITIES for some ladies walking on the HIGH-WIRE of ROMANCE. But there is an OVER CONFIDENCE that leaks out without their knowledge. If YOU can stay EMOTIONALLY SOBER-MINDED enough to walk a STRAIGHT LINE of CHASTITY for a while.

A CHEATERS language has been perfected over time and with the BROKEN HEARTS Nof many women. There is the same air of CONFIDENCE as that of an ACADEMY=AWARD winning actor. Who has separated himself from the mere regular WANT-A-BE's of the entertainment world. To heights only traveled and only arrived by a select few. The key is to stay as OBJECTIVELY NEUTRAL to what is SAID. Then look fir those CONFIRMATIVE ACTIONS. There should always be relative WORDS and ACTIONS to continuously SUPPORT ONE ANOTHER.

When there are patterns INCONSISTENT, seemingly INSIGNIFICANT words and ACTIONS. That is a 'RED FLAG' that you would do well to take into PREVENTIVE PROTECTIVE measures. Meaning... RAISING APPROPRIATE GUARDS. Bring some STIPULATIONS to the table of your AVAILABILITY. Decline some of those spontaneous offers of the WILLY NEELY kind! These are just his PRE-TESTING IDENTIFIERS to see how far YOU WILL GO! Or should I say... HOW FAR HE CAN GET! And... GET AWAY WITH!

Let the phone RING! And when you do... Let some space come between who is the one who says... 'WHAT'S NEXT!' This throws off his WELL CONSTRUCTED CONVERSATION. By a certain time a person of HIDDEN AGENDA has the confidence that his SMOOTH WORDS are like reigns on a horse where all he has to do is give a SLIGHT TUG and YOU will go wherever HE LEADS!

- Question: 'How DO I KNOW SO MUCH about CHEATERS?'

EXCELLENT question! I was wondering when someone was going to ASK? Am I a recovering CHEATER with all this INTIMATE INSIGHT into the mind of the DARK and DEVIANT? Well… I have not lived as a PARAGON of VIRTUE! But far from these individuals we are discussing who go into relations with a total SELFISH regard for nothing other than their OWN PLEASURES! I would venture to say that at some point of GROWTH, UNDERSTANDING and LIFE EXPERIENCES that hopefully every reaches. I arrived at point of personal LIFE DECISIONS of SELF-ACKNOWLEDMENT of WHO I AM. And who I INTEND to BE! Someone who have certain knowledge with the wherewithal to use it for the benefit of myself and others. And not SELF-CENTERED and HARMING OTHERS with this KNOWLEDGE!

Just like little Mr. COOL from my 6th grade class. Those seeds of witnessing those youthful exploits could have turned me into a RECKLESS and UNFEELING person that CHEATERS are! But I believe that a person can DECIDE to become the person that they are according to their OWN TRUE SELF. Or they can allow EXTERNAL INFLUENCES bend them in a DEEP IDENTIFYING way to change them into SOMEONE ELSE.

- Question: 'Are we LISTENING for OUR TRUE SELF and the TRUE SELVES of others? Or are we SETTLING for CHEAP PORCELAIN imitation version of THEM?

*CHEATERS NEVER PROSPER!

One last point about CHEATERS. It may seem like they can GETAWAY with MURDER of the EMOTIONAL type. But while the HEARTBREAK and HUMILIATIONS that they create, they are far from FREE COURSE and ESCAPE. These are the classic 'HURT PEOPLE, HURT PEOPLE'. Their lives are so discombobulated that they will take their own FRACTURED LOVE LIVES and try to piece together some vague form of a REAL LOVE LIFE. Though their major dilemma and SELF-DELUSION is they are in it for the QUICK FIX of the high that is usually a SEXUAL ESCAPE! They languish as the years go by with NO MORE LOVE than from their first disappointing LOVE experience. They tragically drag on from one sad soap opera scene to the next. Never acquiring the LOVE that would HEAL their CHEATING HEARTS!

And the ROAR from our READING female audience shouts... "HALLELUJAH!... That's what they DESERVE!" Maybe so! KARMA does get around. But... the main concern is to those DISMANTLED HEARTS that have become isolationist and VEXED in their spirits. That have become so DISTRUSTING and MEAN that they are now the main reason that LOVE ELUDES them. Their OPEN wounds and SCARS are like an ILLNESS that would infect a would-be suitor. Who when he gets a small taste of a HURT WOMAN'S SALTY tongue and ATTITUDE that he appropriately and with NO WARNING... SUDDENLY STOPS CALLING!

Well... all CHEATERS are NOT the same. Just like all DOGS are not the SAME. There's a tremendous difference from a CHIHUAHUA and a GREAT DANE! One has a BIGGER APPETITE being BIGGER. But they both BITE! However a certain one's BITE is more severe than the other. Here's my point. Some men are FLAT OUT CHEATERS. They are coming in the FRONT DOOR with the FULL INTENTION on deceiving to their ACHIEVING. All at your HEART and MENTAL health's expense. But some men CHEAT from a spontaneous opportunity and are caught up in their own WEAKNESS!

This is in NO WAY an attempt to excuse their INFIDELITIES. But more for the potential of reconciliation in regard to their COLLATERAL DAMAGE. If there's any hope to regain any trust we must differentiate the nature of the CULPRIT. When we generalize ALL MEN that CHEAT as DOGS. We carry along the RESENTMENTS and GRUDGES that will only makes us TOXIC on top of the PAIN given to US from someone that was supposed to LOVE US. Yet BETRAYED US! We would unintentionally limit the possibilities to make future healthy relationships and PERSONAL RECOVERY.

A doctors visit would include specific symptoms of what PAINS and DISCOMFORTS we are feeling, Being exact as much as possible about our HURTFUL experiences gives us the opportunity to find the appropriate SOLUTION quicker than in just a general way. We will also be able to uncover any contributing factors that WE have inadvertently contributed and were completely UNAWARE!

YES!... This is DEEP adult conversations! But the pains that many of us have gone through in our romantic endeavors have left us with PAINS where some still may not have resolved. So if EATING too much PORK, SUGAR, SALT, CAFFEINE or WHATEVER has caused us HEALTH problems of a PHYSICAL nature. Then we should be willing to see what BEHAVIORS, DECISIONS and EMOTIONAL MIX-UPS has caused collisions and collapses within our relationships.

*PRAYER 4 US!

"I'm PRAYING that we will be WISER than any CHEATERS will be more DEVIOUS! Praying that the lessons learned will be heeded and NOT be REPEATED!" ~ A-MEN!

*LIES

Someone once said that a LIAR is the most DANGEROUS person there is! Why? Because they will DO ANYTHANG! Why? Because they BELIEVE and have CONFIDENCE that their LIES will get them out of ANYTHANG! Including MURDER! Yeah... WOW!

Ever been LIED TO? Of course WE HAVE! Has someone LIED to you recently? Don't KNOW YET! Do we? Well... Why LIE? What is it that is so seemingly necessary for a select group of people to put their valued TIME and ENERGY into such a DECEPTIVE OCCUPATION? LIES are defined as 'A statement made that one knows is FALSE with the intent to DECEIVE.' INTENT is the KEY WORD and ISSUE! WHEN and WHERE are willing to investigate the INTENT of a PERSON. What YOU SEE! (Like that OLD SCHOOL r&b classic song)... ain't necessarily WHAT YOU GOIN' GET!

Funny how some will DISGUISE or attempt to DISMISS their INTENT with statements like... "Oh! I was just JOKING! PLAYING! MESSING with YOU! I didn't mean NUTHIN'!" It's not until after there has been the LIGHT of TRUTH and REALITY that exposes the TRUE INTENT. Can't recall any conversations about INTENTION DISCOVERY! So let this be CLASS 101 on INTENTIONS.

- INTENTIONS 101

This is very CHOPPY WATERS that we are SAILING IN... NOW! Being aware and NEUTRAL for keen observation is going to be precarious for most. So let's not make this process any more TEDIOUS than necessary! Someone much WISER than myself said... "If you want to get to the HEART of any MATTER! Do like you would peeling an ARTICHOKE. Just keep asking... WHY? Every question WHY is like another layer being peeled from the ARTICHOKE. So... KEEP PEELING until you get to the HEART of the MATTER!

Not surgically! Nor like a SENATE INVESTIGATION. Just causally over LUNCH or DINNER. A light phone conversation. We HOPE for the BEST and PREPARE for the WORST. There's your BALANCE. Stop leaning FORWARD with so much impatient anticipation for POTENTIAL ROMANCE that you risk FLIPPING over the SAFETY GUARD RAIL. DISCRETION is our PROTECTION! EMOTIONS tend to be the originators for COMMOTION!

Once again TIME and PATIENCE is our ALLY when we allow those components to come in and SETTLE US down before we SETTLE for LESS. Then... more APPROPRIATELY, ask YOURSELF and your POTENTIAL SIGNIFICANT other. WHAT ARE YOUR INTENTIONS? What are the SHORT, MEDIUM and LONG TERM VALUES and GOALS with this person. There should be some sort of VISION in place to GUIDE US in regard to whomever we allow into our CLOSE PROXIMITY.

*STEALS

Just when YOU have learned so many lessons. Our MISTAKES have made us... BETTER, STRONGER and WISER! Just when we thought it was safe to go back into the DATING WATERS! Lo'... and BEHOLD! Here comes the SHARKS! Better known as a THIEF! He who STEALS! Either by STEALTH or by STRUGGLE.

STEAL is defined as... "To DISHONESTLY, INSIDOUSLY or UNLAWFULLY take from another." In our pursuit of understanding. We are dealing with a THIEF of HEARTS. They can range from an EMOTIONAL CAT BURGLAR to the NEIGHBORHOOD GANG-BANGER of the opportunistic kind.

- THIEF by FLIRTATION

Here comes Mr. SMOOTH! The man with the SILVER TONGUE! He is so smooth that he can verbally maneuver like the MAESTRO... Barry White. Then go effortlessly HIGH and MIGHTY like the smooth crooner... Mr. Al Green! Words just melt like butter off his lips. His confidence is his 'RAP'!

He always keeps his game tight with just the RIGHT WORDS! You can almost feel his 'SMIRKING' at you. If you know HOW and WHEN to listen! Pay attention to his VIBE and not so much as to how his SWEET words makes your TOE TINGLES and your HEAD SWIRL. The complicated deciphering occurs because what he is saying has the smattering and ringing of TRUTH! What needs your careful observation is the LENGTH and exaggeration that SWOONS YOU! His VOCAL BOMBARDMENT is a barrage of fact lures he patiently waits for your FIRST NIBBLE.

With every GIGGLE and BLUSH. Here comes another SMOOTH ASSAULT! Carefully and EMOTIONALLY stripping away at your best laid DEFENSES.

- So when are you going to change his subjects from all that GIGGLE and TICKLE?

Where's the conversations of SUBSTANCE? Has he SWOLLEN your head so FULL of INFATUATION, that all you can do is BLUSH and NOD your BOBBLE HEAD? Not trying to be UNKIND. Just being ENLIGHTENING. Mr. Smooth needs to know that you are more than a GOOD OPPORTUNITY with some EXTRA NICE BODY PARTS!

Let some of your LIFE AGENDA be made known! It's all about MUTUAL DISCOVERY and KEEPING IT! If all you're getting is a lot of SWEET TALK than he's probably bringing some BITTER DAYS AHEAD. His flirtatious ways are the tools of his PLAYFUL TRADE. BREAKING HEARTS!

*THIEF by FRACTURE

Just like the MERRY-GO-ROUND. Round and round she goes. Where, when and who she STOPS with... NOBODY KNOWS! Like the 'ol saying... 'He LOVES ME!... He LOVES ME NOT! And picking the petals off flowers to determine whether this is FINALLY the TRUE LOVE of your LIFE! INFATUATION can lead to a PRESUMED LOVE and then REALITY brings the GUT-WRENCHING PAINS of another DISAPPOINTMENT. Then LO' and BEHOLD! Here comes your KNIGHT in SHINING ARMOUR. To save you from another HEART-BROKEN DAY. Your HERO! The one who will piece YOU and your tragic cycle of FAILED LOVE AFFAIRS all back together again... Ms. HUMPTY!

So CHARMING! So CARING! So UNBELIEVABLY RIGHT for YOU! At just the RIGHT TIME in your emotionally wounded life. Like the FIRST RESPONDER at a HORRIFIC CAR WRECK where you were thrown from you're your vehicle with fractures and internal bleeding. Here is someone who will induce the EMOTIONAL CPR and LOVING RECESSITATION that will keep you ALIVE.

Now here is the HARSH and very CRUEL reality of this MASKED BANDIT! He cares for you as much as he believes he can get FROM YOU! Remember ... the main similarity of all these individuals are their unashamed SELF-CENTEREDNESS! Cleverly disguised as CARING, AFFECTIONATE and GIVING. I have personal pleasure in exposing these corrupt minded people who are masquerading as the complete opposite of who they REALLY ARE! I feel the PAIN and hear the chorus songs of those being and have been wounded by men that only care about THEMSELVES.

- Questions: ~ 'How do you know and how can you tell genuine AFFECTION and CARING from the FABRICATED VERSION?

Probably the most intriguingly in-depth discretionary judgment that you will ever encounter in relationships! One that I would not suggest that you dare venture into... ALONE! If there is one thing that I have learned... and LEARNED WELL. There will be those certain LIFE circumstances that can GO OVER our head. We will need more insight than what we can SOLEY generate on our own. WE will NEED GOD'S HELP! My prayer life comes greatly into these types of situations to bring a BRIGHTER CLARITY to our MINDS and SPIRIT!

We need that small still INNER VOICE to enhance, illuminate and bring the needed INSIGHT to uncover these stealthily configurated personalities. You will have CLEARER DISCERNMENT for Mr. FIX-IT? PRAY then ... WAIT! PRAY some more and then WAIT SOME MORE! Then when you get through PRAYING! PRAY! PRAY! PRAY!... and then WAIT! WAIT! WAIT!

Please don't leave your PRAYER PARTNERS out of this very TEDIOUS, yet so necessary process. Why do you think GOD gave them to US! Not always needful to go into INTIMATE details about the intricacies involved. Just PRAY on the obvious generalities and KEEP IT MOVING! Look for CONSISTENCIES! I promise! I'm one of the NICEST guys that you will ever meet! But NICE ALL THE TIME Naaaaaaw! (So keep me on your PRAYER LIST!) But NICE is WHO I AM. That is who I will be on the MAJORITY. So PRAY for INNER SCRUTINY and SENSITIVITY to this person's INNER SELF.

Ask for an ENTRANCE WAY into their very NATURE and FIBER of WHO THEY ARE. If your FRIENDS are available for a quaint and polite introduction. Then ask them... "What do YOU THINK? WHAT DID and DO YOU FEEL? Ask them for periodic assessments and then gauge from WHAT IS NOW and WHAT WAS THEN! Where and WHAT are the CONSISTENCIES... and INCONSISTENCIES? That is where you will FIND if MR. FIX-IT really CAN... and REALLY CARES!

- PRAYER 4 US!

"Thank you dear GOD for helping US to realize that the answers to our HEALING and BROKENESS comes from YOU! That you have allowed us to endure many HARDSHIPS so that we can see our own WEAKNESS and VULNERABILITIES! We pray that this LIFE KNOWLEDGE will reign supreme over our lives from this day forward. We believe that you will bring those wonderful people that will help guide us to GOOD MENTAL, PHYSICAL and SPIRITUAL HEALTH. May we be more VICTORIOUS over every situation that those CHEATERS, LIARS and THIEVES sought to MALIGN and DISSECT us from the BEAUTY of GOOD living that you still have prepared for US!"

CHAPTER 4

'IT IS. . . WHAT IT IS!'

"Whatever people we meet. We can LEARN some LIFE LESSONS from them. Either WHAT TO DO... or WHAT NOT TO DO!"

The wonder of TRUTH is that it brings about a very distinct and undeniable CLARITY of REALITY! What and how we choose to respond will determine where WE GO... and HOW FAR we GO! And with WHOMEVER we choose!

- Question: "What is on the INSIDE of MOST MEN? What's their MOTIVATION? What makes US TICK?

This is just a general background statement about 'WHAT' that many women are never privy to. The INSIDES of a MAN! Certainly doesn't apply to every man. I'm just painting a MENTAL LANDSCAPE for the purpose of a more detailed look at WHERE THE MEN ARE! EMOTIONALLY, MENTALLY and SPIRITUALLY SPEAKING.

- Check the MEN's TEMPERATURE!

Probably the DARKEST side of MEN is the MIND of EROTICISM! Erotic is defined as... 'AROUSED SEXUAL FEELINGS or DESIRE.' These feelings and sensations RUN DEEP If you were to ask a MAN about his FIRST SEXUAL experience, He would have to TRUTHFULLY go back to a time when he was all ALONE. By HIMSELF... with his MIND doing those things that STRANGELY and WONDERFULLY INTRIGUED our young minds even though we could not for the life of us explain WHY? Or WHERE these INTENSE and often IMMENSE desires came from. This is what I call 'THE FEVER' of MEN! We all have it! Wouldn't DARE admit it because we don't want to be LABELED, MISLABELED or MISUNDERSTOOD.

We don't want people (Even other MEN!) to know just how SEXUALLY HUNGRY and THIRSTY we can be... at TIMES! It's that 'FEVER' that comes over US! We could be doing just FINE! Going about our business and daily routines. MODEL CITIZENS, LOVING HUSBANDS, FATHERS and ROLE MODELS in our neighborhoods and communities.

Of course women can sense something EERIE GOING ON! Why you think they SNAP their NECKS BACK so QUICK to SEE... if WE STARING! To see if WE getting LOST in some OTHER WOMAN'S ... WIGGLE, WIGGLE! (FYI...YES!) Those women that be WIGGLING, KNOW EXACTLY WHAT THEY DOIN! And YES... it gets them HIGH (That's their FEVER working on THEM!) with all that SWITCHING making your man and everyone else's man start to TWITCHING!

- First SIGNS of 'FEVER'!

I couldn't have been more than in the 3rd ... maybe the 4th grade. Saturday morning and me watching my favorite cartoons. Man... I was so comfortable and full of my 'FROSTED FLAKES'! Ummmmm! Lying in the middle of the living room floor while my Momma was ironing clothes. Then suddenly disturbing my BLISSFULL PEACE was the shrieking sound of my dear SWEET MOTHER shouting... "BOY!' WHAT ARE YOU DOING?!"

I quickly snapped out of the WARM and FUZZY place that I was in. Then to my immediate SHOCK and EMBARASSMENT did I realize that I had been very SUBTLY, SENSOUSLY and DELIBRATELY massaging and fondling my GENITALS! And didn't even REALIZE IT! WOW! Where did that come from? Is that one of the many discoveries that we first encounter as MEN from within our MOTHER'S WOMB? Don't RIGHTFULLY KNOW! Can't TRUTHFULLY SAY! But, YES it did happen. And probably none of us VIRILE young men could explain it other than... IT WAS WHAT IT WAS!

- The MENTAL MASSAGE

When we can't be there to be PHYSICALLY satisfied. Men engage in the SENSUAL substitution of the ALMIGHTY MENTAL MASSAGE! Where we reach out and close our eyes to the REAL WORLD and go DEEP into our minds eye and can become grossly entrenched in the world of EROTIC MAKE BELIEVE!

From that first image of a NUDE WOMAN that VISION has been BURNED into our PYSCHE ever since. We have not and I am convinced could NOT be the SAME! Don't know the EMOTIONAL levels that women experienced when their adolescent LIBIDO kicked in. But for us MEN it was a MULE KICK! Think about this when you see lil' JUNIOR or MALEEK come in with a 'GOOFY GRIN' that you have never seen.

Probably got his first RUSH of YOUTH-filled LUST from staring at his buddies BIG BOOTY Momma or got a HUG from his BIG SISTA'! Who think's he's so CUTE and her WARM BODY and SWEET SMELLING

PERFUME got him so excited that he found it HARD (Pun intended!) to RUN or barely WALK home.

Now here we have a young teenage BOY who has incidentally or accidently found a NEW JOY and SENSATION that is so overwhelming. That SLEEP was impossible and the GIGGLES and smiles last for days. When he finally starts to come down off this PLEASURE TRIP he realizes that his JAWS are ACHING from all that GRINNING!

This is the beginning of many encounters that FEED our 'FEVER' as little boys that only intensifies when we group up like 'The Little Rascals'. Then someone in that group finally comes clean with their over exuberance and TELLS us all about it. Now for those who have had similar episode we couldn't wait to jump in and tell our own 'HEAT of the NIGHT' tale. And for those who have not been SO BLESSED (So to SPEAK!), will feel LOST, INADEQUATE and INCOMPLETE. This is the beginnings of MALE PEER pressure. And besides... we are DYING to FEEL WHAT THEY FELT... and FEEL!

Welcome LADIES to the back room of the MIND of MEN. I promise there are many men who are not to pleased that I have ushered you in WITHOUT their permission. But the whole significance of reveling who WE REALLY ARE is for our UNIFICATION. If there are MEN out there that are BOTHERED, DISTURBED and UPSET about the TRUTH explained in these pages. Then they are in all likelihood the ones that are the culprits that are in the DARK. And acts like an ANGRY little child being awakened for another school day.

Grumbling for having their atmosphere intruded upon. Who wants the LIGHTS TURNED back off. And the voice calling THEM OUT to be silenced so that they can ROLL BACK OVER into their SELF-CENTERED SLUMBER.

- X-RATED

Men's minds are very subtly assaulted by our surroundings. What was initially a SPARK as a youngster turns into a FLAME. When adolescent adventure and CURIOUSITY have brought us across the path of the AWESOME INFLUENCE of PORNOGRAPHY! The ironic thing about nude adult material is that there is a presumed maturity with regard to a certain age in the proliferation of these materials. Then when the OBSESSIONS of these NUDE images in GRAPHIC and EXPLICIT postures are addicting many MEN'S SOULS. Is proof of and reveals it's debilitating POWER.

With those CHILDHOOD EXCITMENTS that have guided us to a place of PURE LUST PLEASURE. We have found this MENTAL place a REFUGE and RESORT of PLEASURE of the highest form and COMFORT for those LONELY and UNFULFILLED times, PORNOGRAPHY is the place of NO REJECTION! Where the BEAUTIFUL female images can finally be OURS! Under our SENSUAL power and we are FREED (If only TEMPORARILY) from the LOW SELF-ESTEEM that real RELATIONSHIP WORLD can bring.

The addictive DANGER of this EROTIC world is that it creates a VACUUM in the MIND of MEN that cannot be substituted with ANYTHANG ELSE. Even sometimes... the REAL THING! Yeah... WOW! That's how HAPPILY married men with VIBRANT love lives still CRAVE more SEX! We have been seduced to indulge our FANTASY MIND over and over with periodic trips like CHILDREN wanting to go to DISNEYLAND.

The HIDDEN BOOKS in our secret closets, desks, old shoe boxes. The WEBSITES, HOTLINES and favorite VIDEO CLIPS sent by our ol' childhood buddies who still pledges allegiance to our CHILDHOOD FEVERS. Statistics have shared the TIME difference that MEN THINK about SEX compared to WOMEN which is MUCH LESS.

The details behind TRUTH and SCOPE of how much are MINDS have been MOLDED and SATURATED with unending SEXUAL STIMULATIONS would SHOCK the SOCKS off many women. We must maintain our public composure for our ability to assimilate and socialize. But when a man has NOT MATURED and developed MENTAL REIGNS to pull back the BUCKING HORSE of LUST unrestrained! His actions can become very INTENSE and DEMONSTRATIVE!

Our minds have TURNED COAT like BENEDICT ARNOLD and have betrayed US under the influence of UNBRIDLED LUST. Without the RECOGNITION and SURRENDER to a greater force than that of our own willpower. Which is WEAKENED as those SEXUAL MENTAL IMAGES becomes stronger. We would have a better chance of beating MUHAMMAD ALI or MIKE TYSON in their prime. Than defeating that part of our mind that has grown to become it's own IDENTITY. An identity that lies within ourselves and holds us hostage to do it's BIDDING.

Remember... Grand Momma said... "If it don't come out in the WASH! It will come out in the RINSE!"

- Check the MAN'S PULSE!

If the MAN'S TEMPERATURE of his degrees of SEXUAL EXCITEMENT or 'FEVER' needs to be known and understood. Then right in line and very much needed to know is the MAN'S 'PULSE'! His cycle or regularity with his INNER SELF and DESIRES.

- What we want to determine is the MIND SET of a man through his PASSIONS! Why is that so IMPORTANT?
- Why would that be such a determining factor on diagnosing someone's internal components?

Why? Because the SEX DRIVE is such a POWERFUL influence over people and MEN in particular! What I am discussing NOW is rarely ever discussed even in MEN's CIRCLES. YES... we all know that women have regular PHYSICAL CYCLES and IRREGULAR EMOTIONAL CYCLES. But... WHAT about the MEN? Do men engage in subtly unknown cycles of a SEXUAL, PHYSICAL and EMOTIONAL MAKE-UP? This is what I would label as a MAN'S PULSE.

With so much in the way of VISUAL stimulations that create a vast and unlimited MENTAL STIMULUS. What effects then would this have on MEN'S PHYSICAL NATURE? What do MEN do to defend ourselves against the barrage of SEX, LIES and VIDEOTAPES?

- FIRST SIGNS of 'PULSE'!

MEN are more TOUCHY-FEELY than we care to admit! You know it's not supposed to be MANLY to be EMOTIONAL. And definitely NOT SHOWN or let it be made KNOWN! Well... here comes some much needed FREEDOM for all US MEN. I will declare and decree that we now have permission to express what we FEEL... RIGHT HERE! RIGHT NOW! My sincere admonition is to choose WISELY whom we decide to open our INNER SELVES UP TO!

We men do indeed enjoy TOUCHING and being TOUCHED. So much so that when there is no one CONVENIENTLY AVAILABLE. WE TOUCH OURSELVES! We would EXPLODE from sheer overload with a PRESSURE RELEASE VALVE! LADIES… Our bodies respond! I mean respond at an early age. You mothers have already been SHOCKED to see little Taye-Tayes first ERECTION. You can believe you me that our FIRST ERECT EXPERIENCE was SHOCKING! All we knew was that it TINGLES ever NOW and THEN and good for a WEE-WEE! What a delightful THRILL to feel wonderful SENSATIONS when we continued to investigate this NEW GROWTH PHENOMENON!

These are our BEST KEPT SECRETS! Our shame from first PEEING in the BED. Seeing a woman's underwear! Touch a girl and a HARD ON! We wondered… 'Is SOMETHING WRONG?' Does this all happen to other LITTLE BOYS too? And most importantly…' What do I do with IT NOW?!' Some years later or maybe months with this NEWER generation. TOUCHING has become very significant. But there is a dilemma of being a TOUGH CHILD proposing to be a STRONG MAN one day.

We had decided and due to peer pressure to NOT CRY or show SOFTNESS. We mistakenly took those INTIMATE characteristics of our INNER SELF and SHUT THEM OFF and PUT THEM AWAY! Only leaving us with the imbalance of stunted EMOTIONAL development and a very OVER-INVOLVED and ENTHUSIASTIC external self.

We were in atmospheres where GROWN UP literature fell into our laps that STRONGLY AROUSED US. Our 'FEVER', 'TEMPERATURE' and 'PULSE' finally collided and made us so DELIRIOUS that we didn't know what to do with ourselves. So we did what seemed so very NATURAL… at the time like it does NOW! We TOUCHED ourselves.

- MASTURBATION

Masturbation is such a long and clinical word for SELF-PLEASING. It was years before I embarrassedly realized that there was a word for what we little boys secretly did in moments of 'FEVER'. I knew that other little BOYS had to be doing it too! But I was not going to be the one labeled a 'NASTY BOY' by asking anyone! NO WAY JOSE! Then as time continued on with this CLOSET TOPIC that was never talked about. I finally heard someone say something about 'JACKING OFF!' Now mind you... this is like feeling your way around in a DARK ROOM and FEELING for the LIGHT SWITCH or DOOR KNOB. And everything you touch is FOREIGN to YOU. You don't want to call out for HELP. Because you are too embarrassed to have someone very easily open the door and let you OUT and LAUGH because you couldn't DO IT YOURSELF.

I knew it was some sort of street slang. But had NO IDEA it was some SEXUAL REFERENCE! So I did what all little BOYS and MEN do! I stood around and briskly looked like I knew WHAT EVERYONE KNEW! But I DIDN'T! Wearing a MASK at this stage of BOYHOOD becomes very common place. The challenge and grief about it is that unfortunately far too many MEN have not MATURED to be WHO THEY REALLY ARE! And continue the very unnecessary and ADOLESCENT maneuvering of HIDING behind FALSE FACES.

You know us little boys are always trying to build something. I thought that 'JACKING OFF' had something to do with tools. I'm thinking like a JUNIOR MECHANIC and that they're thinking like the ANIMANIAC cartoons. The advantage of women is that women do not let their GENDER IDENTITY keep them in the DARK! Women will ASK... and ASK... and then ASK SOME MORE! Maybe a little embarrassed, but so PROUD when they have gained some knowledge that they know will reward them NOW for any temporary SHAME... BACK THEN!

Understanding a MAN'S PULSE. The very observable behavior in regards to our INNER INTIMATE DRIVE will provide much information and a clearer picture of who this MAN or MEN IS. It will even provide US with an objective image to MIRROR us and share with us facets of ourselves that we can't see. We may have BLIND SPOTS about ourselves where these INSIGHTS will help FREE US. To see what we may have been HIDING from OURSELVES.

How a man responds to his own innate personal EROTIC enthusiasm is different from every other man. No two men are alike. YES! We have much in common where we can LEARN and IDENTIFY about each other. But we have to grow to TRUST and TALK to one another. And also to our SIGNIFICANT ones in our lives as well.

- CHECK the MAN'S RESPIRATION!

The RESPIRATORY system is our biophysical automated system of BREATHING. We do this without the conscious need to 'INHALE' and 'EXHALE'. So what does a person TAKE IN (INHALE) and what do they GIVE OUT (EXHALE)?

- What's their regular patterns and daily routine?

You mean to tell me that you would dare explore INTIMATE WATERS with a person and that you have NOT learned their REGULARS? WOW! No wonder there are so many BROKEN-HEARTED women (... and to your surprise< MEN too!) walking around like the DEAD among the LIVING.

The MENTAL and EMOTIONAL BREATHING that a man exudes should be the DATING ROADS SIGNS to continue, delay or dismiss. Move in the direction from a SAFE EMOTIONAL DISTANCE where he dictates. If you see signs that say 'CURVES AHEAD' then SLOW DOWN and make a CAREFUL and deliberate TURN. If there are signs of INSTABILITY' then that means there is much needed EMOTIONAL 'ROAD WORK' ahead! Which should mean more CAUTION or EXIT is needed.

If you can recall the story of 'THE THREE LITTLE PIGS'. When the three little delicious MENUS to be arrived at GRANNY'S house she was already the WOLF'S APPETIZER! So how does HE behave with his own people before you even came along? How does he deal with people around him (i.e. the waitress, a bill collector calling, a passerby on the street asking for change)? How many GRANNY'S has he devoured already?

When the three little pigs arrived. I was amazed at how they never could recognized their own GRANDMOTHER at FIRST SIGHT? Until it was far too late and almost their UNDOING! Why do women make excuses for those most obvious warning signs? All that STARING, HEAVY BREATHING, SALAVATING and WRINGING of their hands like HE CAN'T WAIT to EAT YOU UP!

What do you ladies call that? PASSION? ENERGETIC? MOTIVATED? YES.... He's all that and much MORE. When we take a MAN'S TEMPERATURE, PULSE, MENTAL and EMOTIONAL RESPIRATION and they come up in the RED ZONE reading. You have a cleverly dressed-up WOLF that is attempting to bring his HIGHLY EROTIC MENTAL world into your REAL WORLD! Like the villainous purser in the 'MATRIX' trilogy who finally was able to leave the computer generated world of CYBERSPACE and cross over into our REAL LIFE WORLD.

- First signs of RESPIRATION!

When a man is HIGHLY EROTIC they have in many ways detached themselves on a EMOTIONAL level in pursuit of a HIGHER LUST level. What the PORNOGRAPHIC mind does is eliminate the TRIVIAL, NON-ESSENTIALS. NO DATING GAMES! No GETTING CAUGHT! NO COMMITMENT TALK the morning after! Just the pure VISUAL SATISFACTION of getting everything they WANT,,, and just the WAY THEY WANT IT! There is a FAST-FORWARD and REWIND button to feed their SENSUALITIES to HIGHER HEIGHTS with just the CLICK of a BUTTON.

NOW! If we take a grown man that has the MENTALITY of a HOT-BLOODED ADOLESCENT with a daily diet of FLESH on FLESH EXPLORATIONS! BAM! What can you POSSIBLY and REALISTICALLY expect other than the GAMES and DISSAPPOINTMENTS that YOU been getting? You've GROWN UP! These CERTAIN ONES (… far from ALL) HAVE not! You have GOALS of SUBSTANCE in relationships! They DO NOT! You have a HEALTHY EMOTIONAL RESPIRATORY system! They are HEAVY BREATHING… all the TIME! Even when they appear CALM. So… PAY ATTENTION!

- TICK… TOCK! GOES THE CLOCK!

TIME seems to MOCK us with all this WAITING! And then WAIT some more. When will the RIGHT PERSON show up? Will they EVER show up is the QUERY that HAUNTS US! We scream on the INSIDE. We have been WAITING!!! When is ALL this WAIT! WAIT!... WAITING going to PAY OFF?!

Well dear hearts! Without the belief that there will ONE DAY be an answer to our prayers. Our despondency would overrun and overwhelm us with indescribable GRIEF. There may already be untold numbers living DAY to DAY MISERY and PAIN. I had to go there so that WOMEN will see that it's not just a FEMALE problem in relationships. It's a HUMAN dilemma that both genders struggle with. What about what US men go through in our search for HAPPILY-EVER-AFTER!

We always hear about the available opportunities that are in favor of MEN more so than WOMEN. So many more to choose from. WOW! ... REALLY? Let's take a CLOSER MALE look and SEE!

- MS. ICEBERG

What about the single parent mother that has committed to better herself through EDUCATION and EMPLOYMENT. Amazingly and to her credit she is raising JAMILA, ZENOBIA and ZACHAREE while getting her B.A., M.A. and taking online classes for her potential PhD. Absolutely FANTASTIC! The REAL life stuff that BEST SELLING autobiographies are made of. Graduated at the TOP of her class. Attended PTA meetings and help with SCIENCE projects while attending little league games and music recitals. AMAZING!!!

She was rewarded with a fantastic job with FIVE figures with the potential for possible SIX figures based on her performance. All the while her very limited time dating guys that just didn't MEASURE UP! FRUSTRATION gradually builds up over time as she wonders... "Where are the HARD WORKING and DEDICATED MEN at in all her SUCCESSFUL FUTURE? TIME appears to be unkind as she LABORS ALONE for so long that there are seeds of ANTOMOSITY quietly being sown.

One disappointing date after another has all but made her throw up her hands in DISGUST! And has driven her to UNHERALDED FAITHFULNESS to CHILDREN, EMPLOYMENT ADVANCEMENT and GOD! "Since I can't find adequate HUMAN companionship. GOD will be my MAN! My COMPANION" is her agony filled retort! All the while her inner sense of COMPANIONSHIP becomes GREATLY OUT of BALANCE!

She dates her RELIGION! Her DENOMINATION and her FAITH has become a substitute for the MAN that is NOT there. Her AFFIRMATIONS of FAITH become a part of her verbal dialogue. When asked how is she? Her response ranges from… 'BLESSED and HIGHLY FAVORED!" to "I'm GOOD I'm a CHILD of the MOST HIGH!" All the while wondering why her LOVING GOD has not sent her that LOVING MAN to LOVE HER. This begins the 'CHILLING' in her SPIRIT.

Now being a GOD LOVING man that FEARS GOD. And a GOD FEARING man that LOVES GOD. I appreciate all my fellow sisters as believers of GOD to the utmost. But did you not sense your 'COOLING' personal and social TEMPERATURE DROPPING? Well… we could feel the FROST as soon as you turn with that FRIGID look when we simply said… 'HELLO'!

At some point you may be expending TIME against you. DISAPPOINTMENT can turn a person into a EMOTIONALLY STIFF person that harbors everything on the inside. Like sticking your hands out to warm them around a FIRE. Yet your FEET are FREEZING! Ms. ICEBERG keeps her HEART WARM for her children, employment and GOD. But much of the rest of the world (… particularly MEN!) get the COLD SHOULDER. When the PAIN of NUMBNESS has set in. It becomes a FAMILIAR PAIN that is assimilated into her COOL DEMEANOR as part of her SURVIVAL MODE.

She quietly and CONFIDENTIALLY (... maybe SUBCONSCIOUSLY) blames INADEQUATE MEN, the FICKLE DATING GAMES and PAINFUL ENCOUNTERS as being responsible for her ARTIC ATTITUDES!

- MS. FLAME THROWER

Very much the POLISHED and ACCOMPLISHED woman of the world as her equal counterpart being, Ms. ICEBERG! Except she is on the parallel end of the 'EMOTIONAL TEMPERATURE' gauge. Where Ms. ICEBERG will freeze you dead in your tracks. Ms. FLAME THROWER will sizzle you in a second on the very GROUND you BREATHING ON.

She is NOT the one to be TRIFLED with. Did I say... AT ALL!!! Well... YES! At A-L-L!!! Her PAIN and DISAPPOINTMENTS over relationships with all it's HURT FILLED misgivings has made her to be the reason that HELL hath NO FURY like HER! FIRE and DETERMINATION drives her to succeed! SUCCEED... however in everything except RELATIONSHIPS. There's ONE great irony about how we recover from PAIN. We can be so well fortified against the very HINT of HURT that we can be OVER GUARDED.

Hearing imaginary FOOTSTEPS in the DARK. With our CROSS and HOLY WATER in hand. Ready to DOSE and DROWN that BIG BAD BOOGEY man lurking somewhere to STRIKE at her again. Seeing SHADOWY figures behind every FRIENDLY FACE and SMILE. Not allowing any potential intruders has cut her off from the FRESH nurturing AIR of REVITALIZATION and a NEW DAY. She is suffocating on her own DEEP-SEATED SUSPICION and placed herself as her own guard!

Unfortunately she has no idea WHAT, WHERE or WHICH KEY can FREE her from her self imposed PRISON. Leaving her with NO way of ESCAPING herself from her own PAIN. She feels no other alternative but to UNLEASH the BEAST of HEARTBREAK onto her nearest recollection of her past mistaken suitors.

It's an INTERNAL RECYCLING of RAKING OVER the BURNING COALS that are CONSTANTLY SIMMERING with her. She is a potential BREAKOUT at any moment. The SARCASTIC COMMENTS! The FACIAL EXPRESSIONS as if... 'YOU MUST DON'T KNOW WHO YOU MESSIN' WITH' can fill the OFFICE LOUNGE or even the FRUIT and VEGETABLE AISLE at the nearby PIGGLY WIGGLY.

And here WE come with our HAPPY-GO-LUCKY selves. Seeing this very LOVELY and RADIANT child of GOD looking like someone we would LOVE to meet and KNOW. Then based on her EMOTIONAL (... or EMOTIONLESS) flow at the time. We could get a LOOK that could make MR. SMOOTH STUTTER! And HE... NEVER STUTTERS!

- FIRST SIGNS of FLAMES

ANGER is the most obvious sign! ANGER with varying degrees. We can cover a person with vague excuses like... A BAD DAY! Something GOIN ON! And of course... HER TIME of the MONTH! OK. But what about the long stretches between the SMILES and the FROWNS. Why do the LAUGHS live such a SHORT LIFE SPAN? Why does it seem there's always something HEAVY on HER MIND? The room seems to be filled with a 'SMOG' of SOMETHINGS WRONG and the FEAR of ASKING about it ... LINGERS.

SLEEP DISTRUBANCES! EATING infrequencies are warning signs of someone that is SIMMERING with a LID ON TOP! RUMBLING and

SLOWLY BOILING! DIFFICULT at best and more likely IMPOSSIBLE to know someone when they are so HEATED UP that they are MAD at the WORLD. Even WORST when they KNOW that their ANGER is causing problems for them and still can't escape it's ANGRY GRIP ON THEM!

- MS. DISCONTENT

How can someone be SATISFIED with someone else? There has to be LIGHT at the END OF THE TUNNEL! If PAIN has gone down so DEEP, than chances are that their level of SATISFACTION is at a very DEEP level to find also. So discouraging to be under the illusion that all is well.... when! BAM!...HELL BREAKS LOOSE through a mysterious SILENT TREATMENT or the COMPLAINT DEPARTMENT goes BERSERK!

No amount of WINE, ROSES and DINNER seems to last long. That INNER PAINS just eats away at HAPPINESS and JOY! It seems that she has already INTERNALIZED another FAILURE that leads to HEARTBREAK and she is quietly preparing herself for what she believes is INEVITABLE. Not realizing that this MENTALITY becomes her self-fulfilled PROPHESY!

- MS. SUFFOCATION

She COOKS! She CLEANS! She's attractive in many, many ways and we would proudly take her anywhere with US. That is until we get wave after wave of daily PHONE CALLS, TEXT MESSAGES and UNANNOUNCED SURPRISE VISITS at your HOME and at your JOB. Excellent HOUSE KEEPER! But cleaning the KITCHEN that's already FABULOUS at 3:30 am in the morning? Knowing that she has to get up for work at 7:00am after she washes 3 loads of clothes is a BIT MUCH!

Absolutely GORGEOUS and certainly one of a kind. But... come on now! All them home-baked chocolate cookies and BABY TALK like we 6 years old makes us feel like we are being surrounded by a room full of freshly baked BRAN MUFFINS with NO MILK or WATER to wash them DOWN... and SURVIVE!

This maybe the woman who is an OUTSTANDING mother with too much MOTHERING in the relationship. It feels like a LEASH of LOVE. Doesn't mean any HARM WHAT SO EVER! Will burst into EMOTION DRENCHED TEARS and hopefully not an EMOTIONAL MELTDOWN if we tried to tell her... ABOUT HER!

CONFUSION and MISUNDERSTANDING could be the FIRE that lights her fuse! Or she may withdraw to a place of her familiar ISOLATION and images of a SPHINSTER running through her head and her inevitable future. Without wanting to HURT her because she is such a sweetheart. Many men will quietly discontinue contact as a polite way of moving on.

But HARSH endings leads these women into a MYSTERIOUS VOID like being lost in the EVIL DARK FOREST. Not knowing which way to turn... AGAIN! NO SHINING KNIGHT! And with no one to CARE and COMFORT her! When all she ever does is... BE NICE!

- DRAMA QUEEN

Me! ME!... ME! It's all about ME! All the world is a stage and WE are merely actors playing in a ROLE that she WRITES, DIRECTS and PRODUCES like the LION TAMER in a CAGE! And when necessary...

with WHIP IN HAND! Usually SPOILED ROTTEN all the way down to her very TIGHT PANTY HOSE! Been the way she is as a little girl who got TREATS and SPECIAL attention for just being... SO CUTE and PRETTY!

Never having the need to build INNER CHARACTER of SUBSTANCE. Intelligent in the ways of the WORLD and very KEEN on MANIPULATION and AGGRESSIVE in SEDUCTIVE INFLUENCE. With out the opportunity to take her LEADING ROLE in whatever DRAMA she FEELS or CREATES. She will fill her esteem with the same NEGATIVE ENERGY... that she DISHES OUT! It seems the BIGGER the stage and audience the better. FAMILY are the first casualties. Then so-called FRIENDS! ASSOCIATES! Passer-bys and even then STRANGERS! The THRILL of being SEEN and HEARD over the most TRIVAL MATTERS (... to US ANYWAY!) is usually IMMATERIAL. NOTHING and NO ONE is OFF LIMITS!

Everthang will be just FINE!... IF we DO LIKE we're TOLD! WHEN we're TOLD and WE will rarely (If EVER) get the WHY WE'RE TOLD! And when WE DO... It's because 'SHE SAID SO!' Living and attempting to LOVE a DRAMA QUEEN will leave you so NERVOUS, FATIGUED and potently SHATTERED that you have become NUMB to the EXCESSIVE CHATTER and NO AMOUNT of ASPIRIN phases you by NOW. We can only change OURSELVES. We don't have the POWER to CHANGE ANYONE! That's up to THEM FIRST and then GOD!

- The TRUTH MAY HURT

OK! I think you all get my drift. YES... I could go on... and ON! Didn't even mention Ms. HIGH MAINTENANCE! Who cares more about her HAIR, NAILS and what you GOT... for HER! Than whether it's a LONG,

SHORT or OVERNIGHT STAY relationship. As long as she's looking GOOD during the duration and coming out SMELLING like a ROSE... (from NORDSTROM'S of course!)

Or Ms. GOLD DIGGER! That special lady that came up with the RELATIONSHIP STATUS of FRIENDS with BENEFITS! After a romantic session and before you can get your other leg in your pants. She's reaching her SWEATY hands out for a RETURNED FINANCIAL FAVOR. A BILL needs to be PAID... (TOMORROW!) A non-paying LOAN. Or whatever her ever-so CLEVER and CREATIVE MIND can declare! SHE WANTS WHAT SHE WANTS is really her ideal of what RELATIONSHIPS are ALL ABOUT. There's NO SHAME in her GAME. All depending on what's in it for her.

Now... so that any readers will NOT THINK this is my NICE GUY way of SIDEWAYS BASHING on females for all the MALE BASHING that is so prevalent and POPULAR. I'm not going into Ms. SACK-CHASER who really needs a REHAB RELATIONSHIP. Or Ms. BOOTY CALL who makes herself available for any man that just might be the RIGHT MAN.

Or even Ms. ALTERNATIVE LIFESTYLE who has put more FAITH in her SAME GENDER to find the LOVE she could not get from the MALE POPULATION. I had to paint a VERY VIVID picture of the male dating panorama so that you LADIES can firmly FEEL WHAT WE MEN FEEL. It's like many women are so caught up in their own DILEMMA of DATING that they are mostly NOT aware of the MALE DATING DILEMMAS. Like since so many men are known to be EMOTIONALLY DISTANT and or DISCONNECTED that there is not much available material for discussions. Well.. that is the very HEART and INCLINATION of WRITING this book.

MEN do FEEL! MEN DO CARE! We are BETTER at PRETENDING that EVERYTHANG is ALRIGHT even when we know that it's FAR from it. We need to LEARN and PRACTICE voicing ourselves more openly if there will ever be a REMEDY. A REMEDY not just for the MEN! But for the needed participation and contributing solutions for many WOMEN'S PAIN and their HEALING as well!

- THIS IS... WHAT IT IS!

Just as we campaigned so VIGOROUSLY FOR EQUAL CIVIL RIGHTS and EQUAL WOMEN'S RIGHT. How we still implore the discontinuation of the use of the dreaded 'N' word. There has to be a GREAT RAISED CONSCIOUSNESS and a PLATFORM for GREAT AWARENESS that results in no less than a vast movement in our HOMES, NEIGHBORHOODS, Community groups and more specifically... OUR THINKING! There must be a better translation of THOUGHT and VOCABULARY with regard to an EVOLUTIONARY change in RELATIONSHIPS.

We are so QUICK to update our relationship status on our 'FAV' social page. But when are we going to UPDATE our RELATIONSHIP MENTALITY? Well... if I never achieve a greater TASK. Let this ONE MAN among the greater masses of MEN speak in a representative way of 'GOOD MEN' throughout our land. That we are OPEN and have long awaited a 'CHANGE'!

- READY! AIM!... CEASE FIRE!

Just like combatants in the MIDDLE EAST who have been waging war against each other since JESUS walked Palestinian dirt roads. We could use a CEASE FIRE of our own. Mind you, that I'm not talking about a TEMPORARY moment to RE-LOAD under the guise of potential PEACE. I am declaring that the AMMUNITION of NEGATIVITY be dismantled like many world countries are with NUCLEAR WEAPONS. Consider and reconsider the sources of our information. Angry MEN and WOMEN! People who have successions of BROKEN and TOXIC relationships.

Maybe we need to RATE individuals like we rate our MOVIES. If what is being said to YOU has a VILE lingering SCENT or TASTE. Then for your own SWEET PEACE of MIND. SPIT IT OUT like IMPROPERLY SEASONED FOOD. Too much SALTY CRITICISM! Not enough CREATIVE PEPPER! We sometimes use more discretion when buying at a 'CLOSE OUT' sale for shoes at our local PAYLESS than we do from what our HOMEGIRLS or MELLOWS are saying.

So... as to not appear or to be presumed to be a WANNA-BE-KNOW-IT-ALL. We have some thought provoking QUESTIONS and COMMENTS from our very OBSERVANT reading audience!

- Question: "Why, when it comes to some things men see the surface but don't get to the ROOT? The PRINCIPLE of THINGS?" *Phoenicia D.- Detroit, MI.

MEN have a certain MENTAL THICKNESS called EGO and UNDERSTANDING! These two components of MEN'S COMPREHENSION are very intimately LAYERED together. It would seem that WE HEAR WHAT WE WANT TO HEAR! And... YES! Don't WE ALL! But knowing a man's overall intelligence is the key to REACHING HIS UNDERSTANDING.

EGO is like the voice in his MENTAL BACKGROUND having private conversations with his CONSCIOUS MIND. Similar to the DEVIL and ANGEL on each shoulder. We develop these character personas somewhere along our search for MANHOOD. Those things that we didn't want to be embarrassed about if we asked someone. So we created an INNER VOICE to TALK TO! YES.. again! Our alter EGO SELF. This was the voice that wanted to say things RAW and UNRESTRICTED at times. But only because of possible HARSH consequences did we learn to KEEP THANGS to OURSELVES!

So you may actually be talking to a COMMITTEE of HIM, his INNER HIM. And the panel of BOARD members of HIS EMOTIONS who are always on the SIDELINE. Just waiting for their opportunity to JUMP into the MIX! Timing has so much to do with it. When? That's where familiarity of KNOWING this MAN is invaluable. YOU have to gauge from that knowledge and past experiences.

- NOTE: "Every OPPORTUNITY and EXPERIENCE has a valued LESSON to LEARN from. If we KNOW WHEN, WHERE and HOW to LOOK and LISTEN!"

The best way to appeal to a man is through his strengths and NOT by the exploitation of his WEAKNESS! *i.e. –"Honey, I know you the MAN! Every bit a MAN! I RESPECT all of who you are! But since we are in this together... I need your understanding ON... ? Can you help me?"

Now! Having to demonstrate TRUE MANLINESS. We have to search from the TRUTH that will bring a better understanding between TWO PEOPLE. Not about AVOIDING TRUTH! True MEN that have developed MENTALLY, EMOTIONALLY and SPIRITUALLY will no longer be SATISFIED with just their SIDE of the STORY. Ignoring RATIONALE and REASON is a STEP DOWN from the mountain of MANHOOD that we GREW to CLIMB.

"It's NO LONGER about BEING RIGHT! It's ABOUT DOING WHAT'S RIGHT!... ALL THE TIME! For EVERYONE!"

Speak words of 'COMPLIMENTARY CONFIDENCE'! *i.e.... "I know that you are a FAIR MAN of INTEGRITY" (BAM!) You just pressed him in a MANLY way that is NON-THREATENING. You are speaking in HIS language for HIM'" with HIM and NOT AGAINST HIM! Men grow through certain test into MANHOOD. INTEGRITY! HONESTY! HUMILITY! (That's a BIGGY!) TRUSTWORTHY! DEPENDABLE! RESPECTFUL! COMMITTED!

These are the levers to pull to get to the HIM that is the CORE of WHO he is and silences his INNER COMMITTEES! This is nothing short of ADULTS communicating on OUR MATURITY level. Every couple has their own and it is UNIQUELY theirs. That's why it's always WISE to talk to the person you are in the relationship, rather than talking about that person with SOMEONE ELSE.

Being REAL will get to the ROOT because we know that when we do that there will be FRUIT when the HARVEST comes. We will certainly need and prosper from the LOVING and NURTURING of our SIGNIFICANT ONE to help us continue the necessary SENSITIVITY to OPEN UP without feeling anything... LESS than a MAN!

- COMMENT: "SOME MEN don't always know how to HANDLE our HEARTS! Aside from REVENGE!"

Let's go back to the little BOYS that we MEN were and remember what we did when we got HURT! We CRIED out LOUD! Grabbed what HURT and RAN calling and looking for MOMMA! If there's one pre-eminent thing that I am imploring you all to get is that many MEN have not MENTALLY and EMOTIONALLY progressed past certain

AGE and DEVELOPMENT STAGES. Many boys are running around in GROWN-UP BODIES.

We CRIED out LOUD! However... that is unacceptable in the MALE CULTURE. So we SUCK UP the PAIN and DIGEST it DEEP inside. That is exactly what we should NOT be doing in many cases. Yet many men do it over and over for a period of possibly many years. There are LAYERS upon LAYERS of HURT and UNRESOLVED PAIN that are deeply embedded inside many of us MEN!

We grab the SORE and DAMAGED areas and to our SHOCK... we realize that we can't LET IT GO. We have allowed this EMOTIONAL CANCER to reside with us for so long. Now IT has us and we are AILING SEVERELY as we make our best attempts to HIDE and IGNORE IT! Resulting in our EMOTIONAL HEALTH declining in SICKNESS without many of us being aware.

Now... to make matters WORSE! WHERE IS MOMMA?! If she is still with US, She may not be available or accessible. She may have her own issues in her senior years. Besides... WHAT MAN WANTS to GO RUNNING TO HIS MOMMA! And may the GOOD LORD above HELP those MEN that DO!

Like the CHILD who was 'HIT'! The automatic retaliation is to 'HIT' back. "You HURT ME.. and NOW, I'm gonna' HURT YOU, BACK!" That elementary mindset is all about NEGATIVE PAIN SHARING. "I'm only giving YOU... WHAT you gave me! The RATIONALE IS... "If YOU hadn't DONE WHAT YOU DID! Then I wouldn't have DONE WHAT I DID! So it's really YOUR OWN FAULT!"

- "When we carefully take our TIME and LOOK at the SMALL things. We can get a much CLEARER VIEW and PERSPECTIVE of the BIGGER PICTURE."

Mark Twain said... "It ain't that we don't KNOW! It's just that WHAT WE DO KNOW! Just AIN'T SO! True in some cases, but certainly NOT ALL! So... how do we KNOW... WHAT WE DON'T KNOW? We have to be better equipped than we have been in our past. Relaying on the same old METHODS and STRATEGIES are only bound to get us the EXACT SAME RESULTS!

We must BREAK our HABITUAL CYCLES of LOOKING without LEARNING. We should be like the SCUBA DIVER who dons his GOGGLES, WETSUIT OXYGEN TANK and FINS.

- GOGGLES

The old saying... 'That HIND SIGHT is 20/20 VISION' is so TRUE! Sight is a very PRECIOUS THANG! It is one of our FIRST and PRIMARY SENSES. But what DO we DO when WHAT WE SEE, ain't WHAT WE SEE? Our GOGGLES are a combination of the PHYSICAL and SPIRITUAL EYESIGHT working together. A diver wears GOGGLES foremost for the PROTECTION of the EYES. When we can PROTECT our EYES, we can PROTECT our HEART! When we can PROTECT our VISION, we can PROTECT the LOVE we have inside US.

Our GOGGLES give us 'CLARITY'! We have the ability to discern what OBJECTS are ahead and in our pathway. Is this someone that I can SAFELY reach out and TOUCH or should I keep a SAFE DISTANCE? There should never be a doubt when it comes to our 'CLOSE PROXIMITY' and 'SAFE ZONES'. When we compromise these initial areas of discovery, we leave ourselves open and vulnerable to UNNECESSARY HARM!

Divers know that sometimes due to the MURKEY DARKNESS of the waters that they need to move at a SLOW PACE. Or even remain STILL to allow for better VISION. GOGGLES will also not allow the SEDIMENTS of MIXED EMOTIONS to distort what we DO SEE, SHOULD SEE and NEED TO SEE!

- WETSUIT

This is the OVERALL KNOWLEDGE that everything that you have read in this book certainly does apply to you. That there must be an OVERALL PROTECTION of yourself when going into DISCOVERIES and RELATIONSHIPS. No FIREFIGHTER goes into a BURNING BUILDING without putting on his FIRESUIT and HELMET. Those garments are worn ahead of time, before approaching any DANGER! Our WETSUIT is the prepared KNOWLEDGE that we wear. And an INSULATED MINDSET when we meet someone while searching for any 'HOTSPOTS'!

We are not invulnerable from people with MEAN and HARSH intentions. NICE people have been known to HURT OTHER... NICE PEOPLE. Totally UNINTENTIONALLY! Our WETSUIT is for those DIRECT and INDIRECT ASSAULTS to our well-being. When we are removed from PRECEIVED HARM and can verify that we are in a SAFE ZONE. Either PHYSICALLY, MENTALLY or EMOTIONALLY, then and only then are we to COMFORTABLY remove our WETSUIT. Without the DISCRETION of APPROPRIATELY DISROBING our protective gear. We would be in a continuously OVER-PROTECTIVE, DEFENSIVE posture. Then there would be CALLOUSES where we are intended to be SOFT and PLIABLE to be able to LOVE and be LOVED!

- OXYGEN TANK

Let nothing stop the LIFE GIVING element of GOD'S sweet AIR from keeping you alive. What do you do when someone crowds your THOUGHTS, IDENTITY and LIFE ENERGY? The precarious thing about OXYGEN LOSS is that it usually comes GRADUALLY! SLOWLY! But very PERCEPTABLE! Then the SHOCK of a MISSED BREATH and the DEEP BURNING of your THROAT and CHEST in ALARM. We need to constantly feel FREE to be who we are. The EXHALE of PURPOSE and CREATIVITY! The INHALING of SELF-WORTH and INSIGHT. The main objective to a valued relationship should be like a continuous 'BREATH of FRESH AIR!'

Not a big fan of prolonged AIR CONDITIONING. Feels GREAT when needed. But it's RECYCLED air that has already been BREATHED with several times OVER! LOVE me some OPEN WINDOW FRESH AIR that has not been through NOSTRILS, SINEWS and somebody else's LUNGS.

Relationships should have a creative way to locate and produce a FRESH VITALITY that comes mutually from one another. Where there is NOT ADEQUATE AIR to breath then LIFE becomes STIFFLING at BEST! COMATOSE at WORST! And then DEATH! Keep your BREATHING SPACES wide and like the SCUBA DIVER. Always have a 'SPARE TANK' of FREEDOM available so that you will NEVER RUN OUT. And not have an UNDERWATER EMOTIONAL EMERGENCY of HEARTBREAK.

- FAITH

I thank GOD every day that 'WE DON'T LOOK LIKE... WHAT WE BEEN THROUGH!' YES, that is a popular saying nowadays. But where do you think that came from? Many a MEN and WOMEN have been to HELL and BACK and like the 3 HEBREW BOYS coming out of the furnace. We don't even SMELL LIKE SMOKE!

There is a DISPLACEMENT of MEN. Many have been LOSS before their time and lived a PRE-EMPTED LIFE SPAN that ended ABRUPTLY. From the STREET LIFE of VIOLENCE, DRUGS, PRISON and IRRATIONAL THINKING. Has lowered the numbers of potentially good MATES, FATHERS, BROTHERS and FRIENDS.

But when the smoke did clear, what we find standing are the MEN of VICTORY! Someone very WISELY said that... "We trade our YOUTH for WISDOM'! We expend years of going TO and FRO in search of PURPOSE, MEANING and so-called SUCCESS (Whether by HOOK or CROOK!). Thankful to have SURVIVED, or maybe PROTECTED from our POOR CHOICES to become BRIGHT and SHINING MEN of FAITH' That unseen PRESENCE of POWER, WISDOM and GUIDANCE that flows through our very BEING. We know that we could not have made it without a POWER greater than OURSELVES, watching over and keeping US!

And HERE WE ARE! RIGHT THERE... in the very places that YOU keep OVERLOOKING! Keep DISMISSING. Maybe not the SUPER FASHIONABLY SHARP guy that you all had envisioned ARM in ARM romancing the STONE together. Inevitably walking down the MARITAL AISLE ONE DAY. But... What's happened to the FANTASY? After all this TIME! The wrapping was TALL, DARK and HANDSOME! But the on the inside there was nothing but those FOAM PEANUT-SHAPED stuffings INSIDE! Not quite the MEN you were expecting!

Meanwhile we men of CHARACTER, MORALITY and FAITH have sat quietly by. Mostly some SHAME at not ... YET achieving our FULL POTENTIAL. Made BAD CHOICES with DRASTIC CONSEQUENCES.

So we had some PERSONAL RE-BUILDING work to do on our own. Regaining our SELF ESTEEM and CONFIDENCE of BELIEF in the MAN and PERSON that we always had believed that we were.

Many times walking and catching buses to WORK at JOBS that received COURT ORDERS to re-mitt HALF of our PAY for CHILD SUPPORT. And because we are MEN of CHARACTER and LOVE for our CHILDREN. We chose not to HIDE under the tables of 'DEAD BEAT DADS' and 'UNACCOUNTABILITY'!

We take GOD from the church and out of the HOLY BIBLE and make GOD more REAL through the LIFE we NOW LIVE! We don't have to FRONT SOME RELIGIOUS PIETY. Just men that have a made up MIND and renewed LIFE with a SPIRITUAL CONNECTION with GOD. We don't feel the need to act like we BETTER THAN! We just NOW KNOW… that we are BETTER OFF than we were before. And maybe ever been at ALL!

WE pray and we live what we say we BELIEVE. If and when we do STUMBLE along the way. LIFE has blessed us with a certain HUMILITY to seek reconciliation and restoration from people and GOD! We don't wallow around in SELF PITY. We are the ones that depend on GOD and live on PURPOSE to keep THANGS MOVIN'

- PEACE

Still waters RUN DEEP! As the OLD SAYING and SONG goes. And so does the SOUL of a MAN that has PEACE. It's an ONGOING and ABIDING daily fulfillment. When there is PEACE on the INSIDE, there will be PEACE on the OUTSIDE! An undeniable aura. An atmosphere that this is a person where their SOUL has found it's RESTING PLACE.

Where there is PEACE on the OUTSIDE, there will be PEACE on the INSIDE! This is not a FABRICATED SENSATION that comes and goes, When a MAN or WOMAN has GENUINE PEACE it is because it has been BATTLE TESTED! Not just some quaint philosophical conversation piece thrown around to impress individuals or the masses.

It's this compilation of CHARACTER, FAITH and PEACE that provides a template of what a MATURE MAN of substance is and has become. And dare I say continuing to evolve. So in the search for this UNIQUE MAN among those WANT-A-BE'S. FIRST look inside yourself. If you were a MAN, would YOU DATE YOU? Many prayers for that SPECIAL MAN has been heard but as not yet materialized because of TIMING... TIMING... TIMING!

"Where are you in your personal area of GROWTH, SUBSTANCE and MATURITY?" I've heard it said that... "Many women want to be MARRIED! But don't want to be a WIFE!" Are all your pre-requisites for a potential mate being provided to them as well? Those distinct POSITIVE MALE characteristics should also existence in you at a FEMALE PARALLEL.

Where there is PEACE there will be CHARACTER. Where there is CHARACTER there will be FAITH! Where there are all of these in your PROXIMITY is probably where you will find the MAN that you have been waiting PATIENTLY and PRAYING FOR.

CHAPTER 5

"OLD SKOOL! NEW SKOOL!"

"Don't let people who KNOW and THINK they know YOU... keep YOU from being who YOU ARE BECOMING!"

I feel very fortunate to have grown up in the TIME period that I did. OLD SKOOL enough to know TRUE WISDOM, TRADITIONS and VALUES. But NEW SKOOL enough to see the evolution of NEW THOUGHT and the FRESH AIR of INNOVATIVE APPLICATIONS. Not wanting our GREAT HISTORICAL PAST that has anchored COUNTLESS GENERATIONS. Through periods of generational ANXIETY and TURMOIL to be LOST or FORGOTTEN. And seeing those seeds prospering NEW ERA'S of great accomplishments that our PATRICARCHS and MATRIARCH'S prayed, lived and died for. That one day we would arrive at better places of EXISTENCE!

- So the question is... Have we fully arrived where we COULD be or SHOULD BE?

And if NOT? WHY NOT? Have we allowed the socioeconomic plight that has befallen and challenged many of us. To consume us and leave us all like TADDERED RAG DOLLS. The ones that NO ONE wants to PLAY with. Having lost our VIBRANCY, ATTRACTION and most of all our HOPE that has carried us and those before us through the WORST of TIMES. Have we permitted in the PAIN and ERRONEOUS thoughts of others that have lost their way? To lead others astray to create divides between the MEN and the WOMEN of our SOCIETY.

- Where are we getting our PHILOSPOHIES from? Who's doing the INNOVATIVE THINKING for us today? To pull us out of the SUBSTANTIALLY LEAST places that we should be in?

- And are we STUCK with the PEER PRESSURE of people who have places of INFLUENCE over us that they have not PROVED THEY EARNED?

Well... I would be a very poor LITERARY WAITER to serve up a plethora of MENUS full of SYMPTOMS. And never provide an ENTRÉE and MAIN COURSE of SUGGESTED SOLUTIONS. Here's the NEW SKOOL, OLD SKOOL REMIX!

- LOVE is the JOURNEY and the DESTINATION!

Where do we LOOK and FIND LOVE? We spend so much energy and resources looking everywhere for LOVE! Desperation and the CHRONOLOGICAL CLOCK has led many of us HOPELESSLY wandering into WRONG PLACES. And we KNEW IT! LOVE comes from WITHIN! We can't give what we don't have! We won't even RECOGNIZE it when it appears if we have NONE of this wonderful gift for OURSELVES.

I can recall LIFE PERIODS of thinking that LOVE came from others as a GIFT and then I would LOVE them back. Now I understand that our PERSONAL TIME without LOVE from others is the NURTURING TIME for SELF-LOVE! We are able to make ROOM and SACRIFICE for others, because LOVE has provided us with a FAIR and LEVEL GROUND to STAND and LIVE ON.

It is not BUILT to predicate what others DO or DON'T DO. If you give someone a RIDE out o the KINDNESS of your HEART and they don't GIVE or OFFER any GAS MONEY. You are not going to be STRANDED on the SIDE of the ROAD... Are YOU? NO! We keep our PEACE knowing that we already have the necessary resources... on our OWN! So... we just KEEP RIGHT ON DRIVING!

Give yourself viable OPTIONS when engaging others. This is how we in a very HEALTHY way FILTER and DEFINE the people in our LIFE. We have many CENTRICAL CIRCLES surrounding US. Those that know us and have EARNED and SHOW consistent LOVE, CONCERN and MUTUAL RESPECT are the ones that occupy THE CLOSER circle proximities.

Our lesser known individuals who have only graced us infrequently and on a somewhat obscure interaction are on the OUTER CENTRICAL CIRCLES. There will be doorways within each CIRCLE to MOVE CLOSER... or FURTHER AWAY as we deem necessary. LOVE is the SPIRITUAL PROCESS that comes from our very SOUL! That is what makes this whole LOVING EPISODE DYNAMIC so CRUCIAL and THOUGHT PROVOKING.

Never ever to be taken lightly or as some form of CHEAP ENTERTAINMENT. When people are HURT, the PAIN can be SOUL DEEP. These matters require a SOUL RESTORING SOLUTION and TIME for HEALING. STOP trying to REBOUND your way BACK into the DATING GAME! For WHAT? To prove some feigned INVINCIBLITY?

What may happen is the creation of CALLOUSNESS over SORES that may LINGER and DELAY the HEALING.

Take the TIMES and OPPORTUNITIES to DISCOVER YOURSELF. Not just as you would in meeting someone for the FIRST TIME. But just as you would someone that you intend to spend the remainder of your LIFE WITH! Because you ARE! When all is said and DONE... YOU WILL ALWAYS be with YOU!

- The CURE for DISCONTENTMENT and LONELINESS is learning how to ENJOY YOUR OWN COMPANY!

Make LOVE WITH YOURSELF! To YOURSELF without RESTRAINT! WHY? Because YOU will be your greatest reference on HOW DEEP your LOVE IS! This will help you see who has the EQUAL CAPABILITY and CAPACITY to LOVE you in a SATISFACTORY WAY... for a LIFETIME!

LOVE is found on the pathway of MUTUALITY. It begins with MUTUAL INTEREST. Then MUTUAL RESPECT. Then MUTUAL DISCOVERY. Then MUTUAL AFFECTION. Then MUTUAL ADMIRATION. Then MUTUAL FONDNESS. Then MUTUAL CARING. Then a MUTUAL DESIRE of a RELATIONSHIP with THEM and THEM ALONE. With whatever time there is for LOVE, JOY, PEACE, HAPPINESS that the GOOD LORD allows.

Look for and follow those SIGNS of MUTUALITY and there will potentially be LOVE along the way and waiting at every TURN and RESTING PLACE!

- The CASE of CURIOUSITY

Without a doubt the person or creature that we think of when we THINK about C-U-R-I-O-U-S-I-T-Y is that 'Dat BURN CAT!' NOSEY ROSEY got HERSELF or HIMSELF in some MIXED-UP TROUBLE just by being a little too CURIOUS! CURIOUSITY has a way of GETTING AROUND to more than just some IMPETUOUS FELINES.

- What about MALE and FEMALE CURIOUSITY?
- Is this possibly an UNTAPPED AREA of INSIGHT that has not yet been satisfactorily discussed and brought to LIGHT?

Is this a OVERLOOKED RELATIONSHIP COMPONENT that is quietly creating some UNDERLYING HAVOC. The type that raises our CONSCIOUS and UNCONSCIOUS ATTENTION in some INDIRECT WAYS. All the while we may never be fully cognizant of this subliminal TROUBLEMAKER inside US? Well... I'm CURIOUS about C-U-R-I-O-S-I-T-Y!

- FEMALE CURIOUSITY

MALE CURIOUSITY is probably so PREDICTABLY BLATANT for you very WISE and WORLDY READERS. That I've decided to take a look at the WOMEN'S CURIOSITY LEVELS from a MALE PERSPECTIVE. ME being ME (ALL MAN and HIGH TESTOSTERONE!) can only share a KEEN OBSERVATION from the OUTSIDE looking in.

Many WOMEN LOVE DRAMA! Earth-Shattering and BREAKING NEWS... I KNOW! But I'm not saying this in a derogatory way like you LADIES have heard UMPTINE TIMES before! I mean when a DRAMATIC tale of INTRIGUE, SUSPENSE and MYSTERY gets your JUICES FLOWING! Mouth TIGHT and EYES about to WATER DOWN the room with ANTICIPATION. Wondering... WHAT IS ABOUT TO

HAPPEN NEXT? This EMOTIONAL ATTACHMENT gives LADIES a CERTAIN HIGH like little else can. We KNOWLEDGEABLE MEN are well aware of this particular DNA SLANT and we use this KNOWLEDGE well and ACCORDINGLY. We have learned... WHEN to SAY WHEN! (Or BETTER... WHEN NOTHING AT ALL!)

But this poor writers meager concern is the SOURCES that feed the FEMALE APPETITE for DRAMA on top of MORE DRAMA! With the current popularity of GUT-WRENCHING and TEAR-JERKING shows like 'SCANDAL', 'BEING MARY JANE' and the 'HAVE AND HAVE NOTS'. There is more than enough OVER THE TOP DRAMA to keep you ladies MENTAL and EMOTIONAL palates salivating for MORE and MORE!

That's where the LINE of FACT and FICTION must be DRAWN! We can EXPOSE so much of our MINDS that we get inundated into a MERGE of TWO WORLDS. Just like the MEN are challenged with those HEATED PORNOGRAPHIC IMAGES. Women can be just as satiated with HI-DEFINITION DRAMATIC episodes of SIZZLING TV MAKE BELIEVE!

Wanting more DRAMA may not mean waiting until that DVR SET night of the week to arrive to catch the next BREATH- TAKING program of TV NIGHT SOAP OPERAS. This where our MODERN DAY URBAN LOVE NOVELISTS sway some of the appetite for more RELATIONSHIP EXHILARATIONS.

Titles like... 'SOMEBODY'S GOTTA BE ON TOP!', 'PAYBACK IS NOT ENOUGH!' and 'WOULD'VE, COULD'VE, SHOULD'VE!' is like the CEYENNE PEPPER that makes the CHILLI go from 'HOT' to 'Oooooow-Weeee'! Our MALE CONCERN is that there may NOT have been MENTAL and EMOTION boundaries set in place while viewing and reading these STEAMY tales of MISCHIEF and RETRIBUTION. What amount of RESIDUE is still LURKING around in those PRETTY HEADS. Wondering if we are involved in the same GOING ON'S that MARY JANE'S co-star LOVER is!

I KNOW! I KNOW! The lady readers are right now expressing with that VIBRANT ENERGY that GOD gave them. Saying... "Heeeeey... this STUFF is based on REAL LIFE! These things REALLY DO HAPPEN!" OK... We GET and GOT THAT! But did that stuff start you to covertly initiate an UNDERCOVER INVESTIGATION over YOUR SIGNIFICANT ONE. As you go from EPISODE to EPISODE and CHAPTER to CHAPTER being influenced by the world of 'DRAMA GONE WILD!'

If so than certain DRAMA STORIES may have the capacity to push a SUSPICOUS MIND over the EDGE! This type of CURIOUSITY can become CANCEROUS and be the ILL-WILL of a relationship that may have been fit as a FIDDLE!

A small LUMP of WONDERING CURIOUSITY can become a TUMOR of DOUBT and DISCONTENTMENT. Before any TREATMENT of COMMUNICATION and COUNSELING can bring a SPEEDY ERADICATION and RECOVERY. YES... CURIOSITY CAN KILL! But only when we allow the DISCOMFORT of INSECURITY and MISINFORMATION invade our RELATIONSHIP HARMONY!

- MALE CURIOUSITY

YES!... YES!... YES! We wonder... "WHAT'S UNDER HER DRESS!" The little BOYS in US that still wants to SNEAK A PEEK can still get LOOSE and RUN around in our MINDS. Reeking all kinds of QUIET RIOTS inside of us while we play it like we 'COOL AS A FAN' and ain't 'NUTHIN GOIN ON'!

Well... is that REALLY A SURPRISE! No MA'AM! No SIR! Like the weary MOM totally exhausted from chasing these endlessly ENERGETIC CHILDREN all over the MALL! We decided to use a 'CHILD LEASH' and STRAP our MALE IMAGINATIONS with the LEASH of MATURITY. Most MEN will never declare how HUNGRY and THIRSTY our SEXUAL appetite can be for fear of RIDICULE and being MISLABELED.

I can recall the dilemma of ASKING GOD... "Why GIVE ME (... later to realize it's a MAN THANG!) such a GREAT PASSION and then have these BIBLICAL and MORAL COMMANDMENTS that restrains us from ENJOYING IT?"

I was SO CURIOUS!... AREN'T YOU? Here's the THING! A MAN cannot completely DENY HIMSELF! When he does he only reduces himself in his own eyes. With this HUNGER INSIDE HIM! This DRIVING PASSION! A NAGGING ENERGETIC CURIOUSITY that would have a LIFE ON IT'S OWN. And would DRAG us around to do IT'S BIDDING. But could it be given as an ESSENTIAL COMPONENT for... MALE HUMILITY?

A man's stature comes from the INSIDE and we take great PRIDE in exuding our STRENGTHS for the WORLD to SEE! But quietly and VERY CONFIDENTIALLY. Many MEN struggle with parts of our MANHOOD that would lead us into a SELF-ABSORBED life of DETRIMENTAL HABITS and CIRCUMSTANCES.

I have always wondered about when the APOSTLE PAUL from the BIBLE spoke... "Satan has buffeted me with a THORN in the side. I've PRAYED three times to have that THORN removed." *2Cor.12:7 The men and women of the BIBLE were living, breathing, heart-beating and bleeding REAL PEOPLE. Just like you and I. Without trying to incorrectly translate something from the BIBLE that is NOT decreed or declared. I would however like to interject this thought simply for the sake of REAL LIFE CONVERSATIONS.

The BIBLE informs us that the APOSTLE PAUL was a single man. He even stated that he "...wished all MEN could be single like him to be available for more of the work of building GOD'S kingdom." *1Cor. 7:7-9 But being a HEALTHY man with HUMAN FLESH PASSIONS and DESIRES he articulated the STRUGGLE that comes from WITHIN!

But being a HEALTHY man with HUMAN FLESH, PASSIONS and DESIRES. I've always wondered (And again this is just my MANY speculations) is that THORN the Apostle Paul spoke of could have been this GREAT SEXUAL DESIRE of men? That DESIRE that many men are so CHALLENGED to TAME!

If it indeed it may have been (though the BIBLE never states what the THORN WAS!) then I can understand and appreciate why the Apostle Paul's response was what it was! The LORD heard Paul's cry and responded... "My GRACE is SUFFICIENT for thee" *2Cor. 12:9 Wow! You mean to tell me that even when we PRAY about our dilemma that GOD will allow it to continue for a GREATER GOOD!... 'YES!' *Rom. 8:28

The Apostle Paul's response was "I will boast in my INFIRMITIES!" *Cor.12:9b "For when I am weak, than I am STRONG!" *2Cor.12:10b Wow! That still STRENGHTENS and BLOWS me away since the FIRST time I read that! GOD knows and HE allows certain PASSIONS inside of us MEN to HUMBLE US. This HUMILITY keeps us REACHING OUT to HIM, who is OUR STRENGTH in OUR WEAKNESSES!

So a MAN cannot reach his full potential of MANHOOD within a relationship WITHOUT a GREATER RELATIONSHIP. GREATER than what already resides inside him. The link with his CREATOR is absolutely essential.

- Why is it that so many MEN DO NOT ATTEND CHURCH?

Wow! This is worth the PRICE of the book all by itself. FIRST of all many of us men may take on CHALLENGES that aren't really CHALLENGES! As part of our PROTECTIVE DNA blueprint we are TERRITORIAL. Our SPACE is OUR SPACE! Maybe that's the VIBE that many women feel before they even approach us with a certain conversation! You can feel that ENERGY WALL that is being projected from us clearly says... "DO NOT TREPASS!"

The biggest issue is who's the REAL LEADER? The feeling of being the SECOND in command to the church leader does not bode well with many MEN. How can someone that is not in MY RELATIONSHIP... or HOME. Regulate my WOMAN and my AFFAIRS. The blood begins to BOIL when we hear... "Well, You know ... WHAT THE PASTORS SAY'S!"

Then there's all the EMOTIONAL FEMALE STUFF everywhere! CRYING, SOBBING and WAVING HANDS all over the place. How can a RESPECTABLE MAN keep his dignified composure under all this ESTROGENE ENVIRONMENT? The INTERNAL STRUGGLE of... "I'm sure this is all NICE and I MIGHT can LEARN ... SOMETHING!" But the feelings of being displaced keeps a man UNCOMFORTABLY DISTANT even when he is there.

There's this MISBELIEF that only WEAK MEN that could not handle LIFE go, that keeps many MEN HOME! Not to mention that all the BEST SPORTING EVENTS are on SUNDAY. ALL DAY SUNDAY! Like many men that have been incarcerated that have a PROFOUND

SPIRITUAL TRANSFORMATION only to lose their spiritual pathway when RELEASED. Many only see the need for CHURCH and SPIRITUAL HELP during times of TRAGEDY or PERIL.

Some men believe that all that SPIRITUAL STUFF is for WOMEN. Like a part of HOUSEKEEPING and making BABIES! True enough that a SPIRITUAL CONVERSION was what brought many men to their figurative and physical knees. But it is a true realization that we all have our own HUMAN RESTRICTIONS and LIMITATIONS. It's the WISE MAN that sees a SPIRITUAL CONNECTION as a great LIFE ADDITION and not a WEAKNESS or SUBSTRACTION to our MALE IDENTITY. This KNOWLEDGE is what keeps us who have made a spiritual transition continuing on our ENLIGHTENED PATHWAY long after the STORMS of LIFE have passed!

- RISE!... DON'T COMPROMISE!

When we SETTLE for less than what we know we deserve. It's like a SELF INFLICTED PUNISHMENT for NOT WAITING for the RIGHT PERSON! That gnawing feeling of ... "I know this person is NOT QUITE RIGHT for me! But at least I have SOMEONE! And SOMEONE is better than NO ONE!"... And to that I say... "HA!... REALLY?" That WEAK RATIONALIZATION has caused many a BROKEN HEARTS!

When we settle for LESS. We are actually WAGGING A WAR against OURSELVES! One side says... "WE DESERVE MORE!" The other side says... "TAKE IT FOR, NOW!" We are ACCEPTING a DOWNGRADE that is siphoning off energy that was intended for the BONDING in a RELATIONSHIP. A relationship with the ONE that we were UNWILLING to WAIT FOR!... BAM! Yeah... WOW!

Now let us take a look at KING SOLOMON of the BIBLE. The WISEST MAN to have walked this EARTH, apart from JESUS CHRIST! He knew that his destiny was to be a MONARCH over the HEBREW nation of ISRAEL. He presented himself before GOD to make ONE GREAT REQUEST! That request was for the WISDOM to lead GOD'S people. *1 Kings 3:6-10.

GOD'S response was... "Because thou hast asked this thing, and hast not asked for thyself LONG LIFE; neither hast asked RICHES for thyself, nor hast asked the life of thine enemies; but hast asked for thyself UNDERSTANDING to DISCREN JUDGMENT. Behold, I have given thee a WISE and an UNDERSTANDING HEART; so that there was none like thee before thee, neither after thee shall any arise unto thee. And I have also given thee that which thou hast not asked, both RICHES, and HONOR: so that there shall not be any among the kings like unto thee all thy days." *1 Kings 3: 12, 13.

What an extraordinary REQUEST and an even greater RESPONSE from GOD! The BIBLE declares in illuminating detail of the GREAT WEALTH and the MAJESTIC projects that King Solomon had overseen. How the other nations of the KNOWN world came to pay homage and tribute to him and sit at his feet to hear his WORLD REKNOWN WISDOM.

BUT GOD!!! Knows us so well since HE is the ONE who made US! So GOD also gave King Solomon ADMONITIONS to be distinctly followed. What were they? GOD said... "When the LORD your GOD brings you into the land which you go to possess..." *Deut. 7:1a "You shall make no covenant with them nor show mercy to them. Nor shall you make marriages with them. You shall not give your daughter to their son, nor take their daughter for your son." *Deut.

7:2b-3. Why was it so profound for GOD to make such a STRONG RELATIONAL RESTRICTION? GOD explained... "For they will TURN YOUR SONS AWAY FROM FOLLOWING ME, to serve other gods:" *Deut.7:4a

Even with GOD-gifted WISDOM and a KINGDOM destiny. It is made clear that a man's WEAKNESS can be exploited through our SENSUAL SIDE. With all of King Solomon's great KNOWLEDGE and unlimited resources of GOLD, HERDS and LAND he still found that there can be a VOID. "Vanities of vanities. All is VANITY. What profit has a man from all his labor." Eccl. 1:2b-3a. King Solomon attempted to satisfy his great appetite for FEMALE INTIMACY by wedding 700 wives and 300 concubine. *1 Kings 11:3. A harem of women on STAND-BY for his READY PLEASURES!

Unbelievable! So to all the BROTHERS who insist that being involved with many women will bring STAISFACTION! The historical BIBLICAL record shows that King Solomon had BEEN THERE and DONE THAT to a degree that we will never even IMAGINE to come CLOSE TO! And to his dismay, he found that ONE can be TOO MANY and 1,000 is NEVER ENOUGH!

Then there's SAMSON. A rebellious prophet from the BIBLE Old Testament who was known for his GREAT STRENGTH and ANTICS! *Judges 13:24,25/ 14:12-14. Blessed with a 'CALLING' to lead the Hebrew nation of ISRAEL as a PROPHET and WARRIOR. He was misguided himself with his FROLLICKING from one woman's BED to ANOTHER! Eventually meeting a woman named DELILAH. Who knew how to PLAY HIS GAME better than HIM and which led to his inevitable DOWNFALL. *Judges 16:15-21.

These men from our historical biblical past have demonstrated how a MAN'S SEXUAL CURIOUSITY. Can then and still does today lead to SCANDAL, EMBARASSMENT, LOSS of DIGNITY, POSITION EMPLOYMENT and most of all PROPER PLACE with GOD! How man of today's GREAT MEN of POLITICS, ENTERTAINMENT, ATHLETICS and BUSINESS have found themselves the VICTIMS of their own PASSIONS!

- THE CORE for CURIOUSITY

So I'm sure that you are wondering why did I suddenly go BIBLE ON YOU? And what in the world does these ANCIENT people from BIBLICAL days have anything to do with US NOW? Well I believe that what we are experiencing in our present day has its origin in those ANCIENT BEGINNINGS. So being a man of FAITH with a POSITIVE perspective from what the BIBLE depicts. I believe that many of our answers can be found when we address the issues that confronted those who lived many, many centuries before US!

"So GOD created man in HIS own image, in the image of GOD he created him; male and female HE created them." *Gen. 1:27. Adam and Eve are the first man and woman that the BIBLE presents. These were FLESH and BLOOD living human beings just like YOU and I. Except they did not know EVIL, PERVERSION or CORRUPTION (... in the beginning) like the world that we now live in. Then GOD blessed them and GOD said to them... "Be fruitful and multiply; fill the earth and subdue it,,," *Gen. 1:28. Be FRUITFUL and MULTIPLY means that Adam and Eve would have experienced the wonderful passions of SEXUAL INTERCOURSE.

All the exciting thrills that come when people indulge their MINDS, BODIES and SOULS into LOVEMAKING! This is important to our perspective because we tend to IMMORTALIZE biblical characters beyond their TRUE HUMAN existence. As if they were MORE SUPER HUMAN than we are! NO! They endeavored in the same human levels of MENTAL, EMOTIONAL and SPIRITUAL activities that WE DO. But Adam and Eve's lives drastically changed. Changed very possibly due to their MALE and FEMALE CURIOUSITY.

"And GOD said... "See, I have given you every herb that yields seed which is on the face of the earth, and every tree whose fruit yields seed; to you it shall be for food" *Gen. 1:29. GOD had placed them in a wonderful place called the garden of Eden. A place where HE has abundantly supplied them with everything that was NEEDED. And I'm sure everything that they wanted beyond their own desires. "Then the LORD GOD commanded the man saying, 'Of every tree of the garden you may freely eat: but of the tree of the knowledge of GOOD and EVIL you shall not eat, for in the day that you eat of it you shall surely die." *Gen. 2:16, 17.

With GOD'S provisions can also come GOD'S prohibitions! GOD had placed the man as leader and caretaker over HIS created earth. They were welcome to be FRUITFUL and MULTIPLY and ENJOY all that this paradise on earth had to offer. Except for ONE GREAT RESTRICTION. The tree of the knowledge of GOOD and EVIL was to be avoided at all costs. And the costs was very EXTREME, that being a DEATH PENALTY! Now as time passes for our FIRST FATHER and MOTHER we are introduced to a very nefarious figure. That creature being a SNAKE among the many animals on the Earth. However, this is no ORDINARY snake. This was a UNIQUE SNAKE like none other since then. This SNAKE had INTELLIGENCE and the ability to SPEAK HUMAN LANGUAGE.

"Now the SERPENT was more cunning than any beast of the field which the LORD GOD had made. And he said to the woman. 'Has GOD indeed said, You shall not eat of every tree of the garden?' And the woman said to the serpent, 'We may eat the fruit of the trees of the garden: but of the fruit of the tree which is in the midst of the garden, GOD has said 'You shall not eat nor shall you touch it lest you die." *Gen. 3:1-4. Now without Eve-bashing all over AGAIN! There is plenty enough BLAME to go around for everyone involved (... as we shall soon see). Eve had not seen any other SNAKES or animals of any kind that could SPEAK. Maybe that was ONE of her FIRST CURIOUSITIES that diverted her from her RIGHT COURSE and RIGHT PLACE.

Do important for us to always consider and re-consider our sources. No matter how DISTINCTIVE they may appear. The TRUTH as declared by GOD should always be our determiner of WHAT to RECEIVE and WHAT to REJECT! "Then the serpent said to the woman, 'You will not surely die. For GOD knows that in the day you eat of it your eyes will be opened, and you will be like GOD, knowing GOOD and EVIL." *Gen: 4,5. CURIOUSITY can usually lead to DOUBT. DOUBT is that negative vibe that leads us astray from TRUTH! Now Eve is CURIOUSLY wondering if this RARE creature is enlightening her on something that Adam and even GOD HIMSELF did not want her to know!

- EVE'S DILEMMA

Could it be that there is an inbreed DNA gene that was intended to facilitate women in their role as FEMALE, WIFE and MOTHER. That somehow through EVE's indiscretion has been MISUSED and even possibly PERVERTED? Inquiring minds WANT TO KNOW! But CURIOUSITY can lead to DOUBT! That LAGGING and WANDERING FEELING of somehow being left behind! An undeclared, unpublicized OUTCAST that everyone knows about but NO ONE will say it OUTLOUD! An inner gnawing that was planted by a SEED of NEGATIVITY.

Eve's gift of a FREE-WILL and FREE THINKING mind was assaulted by words from a stranger against the ONLY people that she KNEW and LOVED! Her own FAMILY! The old saying goes... 'That a STRANGER cannot get CLOSE ENOUGH to HARM or HURT US... like someone who is CLOSE! SOMEONE WE TRUST! Like the DOUBT that I'm sure captivated EVE, can soon bring another NEGATIVE companion like FEAR. What do we do when the very things that we have TRUSTED IN and believed were challenged as NOT TRUE. Then what do we DO? Where do we GO?

Woe unto US when we see an ENEMY as a FRIEND. And a FRIEND as an ENEMY! Then ABANDONMENT finds an open door that FEAR has swung WIDE! Feelings of BETRAYAL of those we TRUSTED have left far too many of us in MONUMENTAL DISARRAY and potentially UNGUARDED. Not being ABLE to TRUST our own JUDGEMENT, INSTINCT and DISCERNMENT.

- ADAM'S DILEMMA

"... she took of the fruit and ate." *Gen. 3:6b. So what did our great leader ADAM who was the ONE who first knew and fellowshipped with GOD do? What did our HERIOC MAN of the moment do while all this was taking place? "... she also gave to her husband with her, and he ate" *Gen. 3:6c. HOLD ON! Wait a COTTON-PICKING minute. Isn't this the part of the story where our ORIGINAL FATHER was supposed to show all that MANHOOD and STRAIGHTEN EVE and that SNAKE OUT? About what... 'THUS SAY'S THE LORD?!'

Apparently this situation exposed some potential doubts of Adam as well. By Eve giving the fruit to Adam after she ate would give cause to believe that Adam was possibly present during Eve's and the snakes whole TRAGIC conversation. And stood in SILENCE and DID NOTHING! This is the character defect in Adam that seemingly has infected many a men today. He willingly played the part of MR. INSIGNIFICANT to see what if anything would be the outcome. Something that maybe he theorized that perhaps GOD withheld from him.

So we see Adam and Eve meeting on common ground. Unfortunately it was 'SHAKY GROUND'! We have allowed ourselves to become so SILENT as almost unnoticed and so INACTIVE as almost NON-EXISTENT! Deep on the inside of every MAN and WOMAN there needs to be a spirit of a POSITIVE SELF. To breed the unprecedented quality of STRENGTH and COURAGE to resolve come what may!

Adam allowed himself and his LEADERSHIP role to be DISMISSED by an outside source. This is why I believe that during a MARRIAGE ceremony it is understood that there should be... NOTHING that COMES BETWEEN HUSBAND and WIFE.

- ARE WE THE ADAM AND EVE OF OUR DAY?

"Then the eyes of both of them were opened, and they knew that they were naked: and they sewed fir leaves together and made themselves coverings." *Gen. 3:7. DOUBT can and has led many of us into DESPERATE THINKING and DESPERATE MEASURES! There is no worse feeling than to OVER RE-ACT to a situation that we were so sure of. Only to find out that the situations was not at all, what we thought it was. And then to realize that our OVER-REACTION contributed to the episode worsening. DOUBT erodes what once was or could have been a firm foundation of FAITH! Science has declared... 'That NO TWO OBJECTS can occupy the SAME SPACE!' Either we will have FAITH and believe TRUTH or we will DOUBT and be led astray.

Have we left ourselves vulnerable due to lack of allegiance to TRUTH! The same TRUTHS that GOD has presented to the FIRST MAN and WOMAN. Then rationalized multiple options in our search to be like GOD who knows ALL THINGS! Or at least enough things to JUSTIFY living with what is right in our own eyes. Then we suffer through FAILED RELATIONSHIPS seemingly BACK to BACK! One RIGHT after ANOTHER! We swear UP and DOWN and even on dear SWEET MOMMA's GRAVE... that we will DO BETTER! And what happened that LAST TIME... won't NEVER... EVER, NEVER HAPPEN AGAIN! Only to be re-visited with more fractures to the HEART and DEEPER DISAPPOINTMENTS!

We cover our NAKEDNESS of STUBBORNESS and LACK of FORESIGHT with coverings of FINGER POINTING and DENIAL. As we search for our next HOSTAGE to be or someone else's VICTIM that is HURTING more than WE ARE! Our eyes have been OPENED to GOOD and EVIL. But we are still blindly trying to impose our WILL on LIFE CIRCUMSATNCES and anyone in our CLOSE PROXIMITY. "Then the

LORD called to Adam and said to him, 'Where are YOU?' Adam and Eve's greatest failure was their SELF-INDULGENCE to want more than GOD gave. They left GOD out of this CRUCIAL time and event in their LIVES! Is this the same tragedy being relived today in our LIVES?

- THE CURE FOR CURIOUSITY!

"Also for Adam and his wife the LORD GOD made tunics of skin, and covered them" *Gen. 3:21. I have come to believe that there are many things available to us that would benefit us in monumental ways. "If any man lacks WISDOM, let him ask GOD, who gives to all liberally and without reproach, and will be given him." *James 1:5. We certainly need WISDOM in these last and perilous times. No one intentionally wants to walk around being the CLASS DUNCE or DUMMY to the world.

*So how is it that so many who believe in GOD and HIS truth, keep coming up LACKING in the area of relationships?

*Why then is it so DANG-BLASTED HARD to find that JUST RIGHT person... let alone our SOUL MATE?

I'm so reminded of King Solomon's prayer request when he prayed to GOD for WISDOM to lead the nation of Israel as their King. GOD was so impressed with his appeal that he blessed him with so much more than he ASKED for! * 1Kings 3:11-13. But at the end of his life King Solomon's reign had become a major disappointment to GOD. Because he had allowed the WRONG SOURCES to have influence over him. That influence rendered his FAITH IMPOTENT!

I can also see from the life of King Solomon that WISDOM is NOT the ultimate in virtues desired. I believe that if King Solomon had requested PRESERVERING FAITH that the same WISDOM he received would have also been GRANTED. FAITH is the MUZZLE that quiets the constant BARKING of CURIOUSITY and DOUBT. The LORD JESUS himself was not so easily impressed with just KNOWLEDGE alone. Especially when dealing with US... FICKLE human beings. But the BIBLE proclaims that it was an unwavering act of FAITH that IMPRESSED and AMAZED even our LORD JESUS~ *Luke 7:7-9

Our FAITH cannot be regulated by TIME or CIRCUMSTANCES. These are the times that are FAITH is SEASONED and MARINATED like the choicest of SIRLOIN STEAKS. GOD is indeed 'PREPARING US' like that great gospel song powerfully sung by DARYL COLEY and the Wilmington/Chester Mass Choir. FAITH is our LIFELINE that attaches us to an UNSEEN DESTINY. When we don't BELIEVE... WE FAINT! FAITH is the BAROMETER of our SOUL'S condition. You want to know where a person is in their SPIRITUALITY? Just pay attention to the way they LIVE. In the GOOD TIMES and SEASONS and certainly in the DIFFICULT DAYS and DROUGHTS. Our success in LIFE and RELATIONSHIPS are all connected inexplicably with our FAITH!

- LAYERING

GOD has put a very special person into my life. That person being Dr. MARILYN BAILEY who is the director of the 'Early Childhood Development' curriculum at the University of Arkansas at Pine Bluff (UAPB). Dr. Bailey conceived a penetrating human dynamic for her doctorial thesis called 'SHOULDERING'. In that concept she described how we human beings may knowingly or unknowingly come into a sustained relationship based on needed support or BRIDGING for stability.

Using her human characteristic reflection as a reference. Advancing this brainchild further I have come to see that a healthy relationship builds and BONDS through 'LAYERING'. We try so intently to see if we are the 'BIRDS' of a feather that FLOCK together or indeed if we are the OPPOSITES that ATTRACT.

I surmise that there are times in our INDEPTH ANALYSIS of almost everything. That we sometimes are GUILTY of OVER THINKING our realities. Sometimes by maybe the SUBTLE and UNCONSCIOUS way we attempt to ascribe ourselves to what we attempt to FABRICATE. Rather than just be WHO and WHAT we really BE! This goes for others in our relationship SURROUNDINGS as well.

So burning is our search for LABELING one another with our URGENCY to NOT let another FISH OFF the HOOK. That we actually contribute to BLURR our lines of VISION. We adhere to a perception based on... 'WHAT WE WANT SOMEONE TO BE'. And then COOPERATE in an attempt to MOLD them without their PERMISSION. LAYERING is a coming together as you are and finding the CHARACTERISTIC and INTIMATE grooves and CURVES of someone's PERSONALITY and MENTAL/EMOTIONAL makeup. Then we can decide if this is someone that I can PUT UP with or PRETEND WITH!

LAYERING is a building process where the BLUEPRINT is only EXPOSED as YOU BUILD. That's a GOOD THING, because it calls for PAUSES and REFLECTIONS. Keen OBSERVATIONS and INTERSPECTIVE STUDYING. Remember the CORE element of RELATIONSHIP. Allowing someone into the most SENSITIVE part of your being. Your HEART! Your MIND! Your SOUL! This undoubtedly should be a progressive process. If you can't comfortably PASS the TEST of someone's MIND'S SECURITY and SCRUTINY. Then there's no way on GOD'S GREEN EARTH and

BLUE SEAS that you can expect to get to someone's HEART! So quite naturally the SOUL is COMPLETELY OUT OF THE QUESTION!

LAYERING provides us with an OBJECTIVE process where we can confirm our PRECEPTIONS and create a necessary EXIT or DISMISSAL when appropriate. LAYERING is a primary process of 'THE TWO BECOMING ONE'! Where we become MENTALLY BI-LINGUAL with one another. The comfort zones began to OVER-LAP and you can finish each other's statements. As well as know when to call or reach out to the other due to a MUTUAL VIBE that resides in each other.

Like matching outfit apparel and accessories together. We look at... step back and even turn around to see if what we're wearing fits what we have in MIND. How we want the world at large to see US. And how it all fits into our MOOD and MODE of DRESS for the day. It's the ROAD that leads us to COMMON GROUND. That's why and HOW BIRDS NOT of the SAME FEATHERS... can HAPPILY co-exist and FLOCK TOGETHER. This is the points of where GENUINE AFFECTION comes into play. When we are GROUCHY and having a GRUMPY day. We have someone who understands us and has the EMOTIONAL wherewithal to allow us that space we need. Without letting US RUIN their day! They KNOW WHO WE ARE! These are people who are LAYERED to and WITH US. So they know OUR GROUCHY days. The BONDING CONNECTION allows them to LOVINGLY wait on us to return BACK to WHO WE FULLY ARE.

LAYERING also creates a SKIN of protection around people who are in this BLENDING PROCESS. While BLENDING and BONDING the primary individuals together it tends to keep OUTSIDERS, INTRUDERS and SPECTATORS at BAY and OUTSIDE. Like our skin that thrives with MOISTURE.LAYERING needs ATTENTIVE CARE and COMPASSION to keep it's SUPPLE TEXTURE ALIVE

- CHEMISTRY

As the LAYERING process continues to evolve. It initiates another process of 'CHEMISTRY'. It can be 'TAP WATER' from the ROCKY Mountain High or it can be some 'HOLY WATER' straight from the ALTAR. But when you mix either one with... OIL. You goin' get SEPARATION! SHAKE! SHAKE! SHAKE! All you want like K.C. and his Sunshine Band. But I promise you that when you sit those NON-COHESIVE elements DOWN. They will SEPARATE... EVERY TIME!

CHEMISTRY is a TRUTH reality that cannot be DENIED. TIME will prove this repeatedly, over and over. We can GRIT our TEETH and CLINCH our FIST for so long in our attempts to conform to someone else's desires. But... Oooooh BOY! When the POT has been on the stove to long with the LID about to BLOW OFF from someone feeling RESTRICTED in a relationship. We will clearly see for ourselves... ONCE AGAIN that a LEOPARD cannot change it's SPOTS!

We can all find areas to IMPROVE in and that can make things better and LIFE more bearable. But who a person is at their CORE is who they will be in their ESSENCE. CHEMISTRY is that very OBSERVABLE element where we can distinguish the different TONES and HUES of an individuals personality.

- How well does individuals MIX? Are there points where it 'DON'T MIX WELL... or NOT AT ALL?

- Is that something that can or should be TOLERATED, EXCUSED or COMPENSATED for?"

Someone wisely said... "That if you meet someone that did something that really ERKKED your NERVES. And that person NEVER CHANGED. Would you be able to HANDLE IT?

- KEYS TO CHEMISTRY

Without a DOUBT! UNDERSTANDING is the MAIN INGREDIENT for HEALTHY CHEMISTRY. We would do well to take into consideration of the varying degrees of RELATIONSHIP CHEMISTRY. There is the INTRODUCTORY level of CHEMISTRY. Where the majority of time spent is like the RESEARCH PHASE. Where the discovering is the thing. This is the CRUCIAL phase of DISCOUNTING or VERIFYING the objective evidence of WHAT we KNOW from WHAT WE THINK! And... WHAT WE THINK WE KNOW!

TRUTH is that our disappointments come in the early stages of KNOWING someone because they may not be who they presented themselves to be. Or we have discovered that we may have ascribed attributes to them that were more of our FANTASY PERSON than the REAL THANG! One of the most DISTORTING and DAMAGING activities that THROW objectivity straight out the window is the ONE NIGHT STAND! A QUICKIE! Pre-mature sexual activity can put our EMOTIONAL CART before our LOGICAL HORSE. We have just discombobulated our RESEARCH and DISCOVERY of another relationship whenever we become pre-maturely SEXUALLY INVOLVED.

Then there are the intermediate levels of CHEMISTRY where there is evidence of CHARACTER TRUTH and IDENTITY CLARITY of each individual. The last thing any CHEMISTS wants to do is USE and MIX ELEMENTS that are UNKNOWN and UNLABELED! That's why a

SUCCESSFUL CHEMISTS has peers to do their ANALYISTS for the sake of CONFIRMATION. We need individuals in our lives to help us SEE what maybe WE ARE TOO CLOSE to SEE for OURSELVES.

I would suggest that when TRUE CHEMISTRY is CONFIRMED and VERIFIED. Then we know that we are working with something of LASTING and LONG VALUE. A relationship with HEALTHY CHEMISTRY provides US the BASE ELEMENTS to build on INDIVIDUALLY and TOGETHER within the relationship. One of the SUCCESSFUL SIGNS of GOOD CHEMISTRY is the dramatic effect on a person SOCIALLY, PROFESSIONALLY and RELATIONSHIP-WISE. With FAMILY, FRIENDS and even those who are ACQUAINTANCES or STRANGERS.

The CHEMISTRY of individuals in a LOVING RELATIONSHIP creates a VIBE that we have come to know as ‘GLOW’. And a SWEET SONG in the SPIRIT that is expressed through JOY, PEACE, SERENITY and BALANCE. When a person is LOVED fully this nurturing enhances all of who that person is. There is a ALTITUDE of LIVING that becomes FULL OF LIFE. The juxtapose dynamic of this PLEASURABLE LIFE is the one with an UNHEALTHY CHEMISTRY. Where a person’s LIFE ESSENCE is DIMINISHED and where there should be a ‘GLOW’. There is the ‘DULL’ darkness of a person SUFFEREING and TRAPPED in MISERY to someone that DOEST NOT LOVE THEM.

NEVER EVER let DESPERATION to be with someone take you to a LESSER place of PAIN and SORROW. In the illusion that maybe one day things will get BETTER. Things will get better for YOU when you LEAVE someone that MISTREATS YOU and does NOT APPRECIATE YOU. Then you can HEAL and LOVE and let others LOVE YOU. Until the day when LOVE TRULY does come to YOU!

Apart from our GOD CONNECTION this is the HIGHEST CHEMISTRY that there is in LOVING YOURSELF. This is a GIFT given by GOD. When we venture into our journey for LOVE I have found that LOVE comes from GOD and that HE... HIMSELF is LOVE! We have aimlessly pursued LOVE within the framework of our own KNOWLEDGE and DIRECTION. Which we have found FAILED! Then there are those of us who do believe that GOD is LOVE and will BLESS US... ONE DAY! But, HONESTLY... WHY IS IT TAKING SO LONG?

And I will gladly share these thoughts of LOVE and CONCERN with you. But the consummate outcome will more than likely hinge on... "WHAT DO YOU BELIEVE?"

CHAPTER 6

'DO YOU BELIEVE?'

"Many relationships FAIL when we attempt to UNITE with a PERSON and NOT... EMBRACE their SOUL!"

In so many ways we are our OWN DESTINY. What we THINK, SAY and BELIEVE molds a great deal of WHO we are and tends to lead the way we GO. Our THINKING influences so much of WHAT we BELIEVE. And equally so and maybe more... what we BELIEVE influences what WE THINK! What we SAY reveals BOTH!

What we BELIEVE is the most INFLUENTIAL MENTAL and EMOTIONAL characteristic of OUR CORE BEING. Our SOUL or INNER SELF is deeply immersed in our FAITH and BELIEFS. Whether we attempt to remain NEUTRAL in certain decisions or LIFE INSTANCES. That NEUTRAL decision is in of itself comes from a BELIEF SYSTEM of how our thoughts gravitate together.

The most catapulting component that drives us or derails us is based on our MINDSET! We can choose which INNER ENERGY propels us through POSITIVITY, NEGATIVITY or UNCERTAINTY!

- NEGATIVITY

Like the immensely depressed character from the FLINTSTONES known as 'SCHLEPT ROCK,' always bemoaning the futility of anything GOOD and POSITIVE. The NEGATIVE MINDSET refuses to BELIEVE that the SUN will SHINE again. That there will be a HAPPY ENDING and that the HERO will come to the rescue in the NICK of TIME and SAVE THE DAY.

NEGATIVITY drains the very LIFE essence from individuals and everyone around them. It's like having the OXYGEN sucked out of the room and not being able to BREATH. The NEGATIVE MIND restrains and DENIES those things that could bring a possible CHANGE for the better.

It's as if a person has been down for so long that they see no sense in making any further attempts in getting back up! That all HOPE has been lost and it's better to accept a DISMAL FATE and begin to accept the inevitable PAIN. Than to be DISAPPOINTED when the UGLY and DARK CYCLE continues again and again.

NEGATIVITY is a POISONOUS SEED that grows vines of DISTRUST that eventually STRANGLES all HOPE AWAY. I believe that we witness such UNHAPPY SOULS in their latter years. When NOTHING seems to remove their WRINKLED FROWN that has been lodged and etched in their SAD FACES over the years. SHORT and FRUSTRATED WORDS come in their responses and comments that have us shaking our HEADS. As we wonder what could have happened to them that has made them this way?

What happened was their inability to RESOLVE LIFE on LIFE TERMS. That LIFE had not SINGLED them out as it's PERSONAL PUNCHING BAG and they were GOOD- FOR-NOTHING ELSE. The NEGATIVE

MINDSET is like someone who has driven OFF the MAIN ROAD of LIFE. And are RUMBLING along with much AGITATION on the SHOULDER of the ROAD.

Without a DRASTIC change of MENTAL COURSE they will surely drive themselves into an 'EMOTIONAL DITCH' that will be very difficult to come out of. And possibly take many PRECIOUS DAYS, WEEKS, MONTHS and YEARS of LIFE that are intended to be lived with VIBRANCE and VITALITY.

- SIGNS OF NEGATIVITY

It doesn't take long and it certainly doesn't take much to find the 'NEGATIVE' one out of the CROWD. There is a sense of a 'DARK CLOUD' hanging over them in their atmosphere. SHORT WORDS feel like a 'CAR CRASH', 'TRAIN WRECK' and a 'STUBBED TOE' rolled into ONE! This is where a person's INNER BELIEFS can come into play. There has got to be a TRANSFORMATION of THOUGHT LIFE! It's like a 'CODE BLUE' alarm in the hospital where someone's LIFE is on the LINE.

We are made up of three components that make up a WHOLE PERSON. We are MIND, SPIRIT and BODY. Just like our governmental system where we have a CHIEF of STATE, SENATE and CONGRESS. This is to ensure a corrective sense of BALANCE for efficient national operation.

So we need to employ all who we are for NECESSARY BALANCE and CORRECTION. When a person is overwhelmed with a NEGATIVE MINDSET there likely has been unresolved issues where the MIND and SPIRIT were held HOSTAGE. This is where we have to inventory ourselves and SEEK resources that build our SPIRITUAL SELVES UP and move our BODIES to the appointed places of COUNSELING and SUPPORT.

PHYSICAL HEALTH and exercise can provide needed ENERGY to fight off any NEGATIVE INVASIONS. Without a CHANGE we become our own prophet of SELF-DEFEATED DOOM! WE ARE WHAT WE BELIEVE! Even if it's NOT for our OWN GOOD! And can contribute to our OWN SELF-DESTRUCTION. NEGATIVITY is like DAILY SUICIDE one THOUGHT at a TIME. Don't let NEGATIVITY RIDE into your LIFE. When NEGATIVITY RIDES... sooner or later, NEGATIVITY will want to DRIVE!

- UNCERTAINTY

These are the ones that POLITICAL CANDIDATES look to impress before the polls close and consider them as their potential 'SWING VOTE'. The ones who would prefer to play everything SAFE until they can get an IRON CLAD, NO FRILLS GUARANTEE. That LIFE is NOT going to HURT or TRICK THEM... ANYMORE! The BLUE SOCK or the BROWN? Should I part my HAIR or just COMB it to the BACK. The ongoing MENTALITY of constantly recycling the most TRIVIAL ideas tends to leave them at a SLOWLY SINKING STAND STILL!

And so with their LOVE LIFE or should I say LACK OF LOVE LIFE. Their idea of dating are PAINFULLY long spells of INACTIVITY and COMPLACENCY as they sway in their WALL FLOWER dance. Waiting for someone to finally ask them out. Only to miss another opportunity to venture to LOVE due to their STALLING and DELAYING. Contemplating what WOULD or WOULDN'T happen. With much ANXIETY exclaiming that most CERTAINLY NOTHING USUALLY DOES.

Having heard so many HORROR stories of SOUR episodes of 'LOVE GONE WRONG'. There is that ANNOYING voice inside them telling them to just STAY IN their corner and PRAY, MEDITATE or just continue to IMAGINE what one day... COULD BE. The most promising part of an UNCERTAIN MENTALITY is that they have a 50/50 chance to go either way. At some point in their journey they may connect with a FRIEND, POSITIVE VIBE, INFLUENCE or GROUP that pulls them out of their MENTAL MUD of INACTIVITY.

The challenge for the one who has been coerced by UNCERTAINTY is the potential of falling back into their FAMILIAR FRAME of DOUBT. We all can revert back to what is FAMILIAR! We have become so comfortable with things that may not be reasonable. But we have adjusted ourselves to FIT in them and learned to GRIN and BEAR IT.

- POSITIVE

Thank GOD for BRIGHTER DAYS! For a NEW DAY. One where the DARK CLOUDS have all been PUSHED and ROLLED AWAY. No it didn't just happen by CROSSING our FINGERS and HEARTS and making WISHES. We continued to BELIEVE in what is GOOD. What is RIGHT and REFUSED to ACCEPT anything LESS. Even through our TEARS, FEARS and with ANXIETIES... CREEPING IN. We NEVER GAVE UP! The energy of POSITIVITY has a REGENERATING component. It becomes a SELF-SUSTAINING force of LIFE that contributes itself to it's HOST (... that BE, YOU and I) and will NOT SURRENDER, change COURSE or DIE.

How do you possibly think that we of our own LIMITED HUMAN SELVES could overcome all of our personal STRUGGLES and BATTLES? I'm talking about those stories that only a few precious souls in our CIRCLES... KNOWS. The rest we are content to take to our GRAVE and share with GOD and GOD ALONE. The element of POSITIVITY requires us to SEEK more WISDOM about WHAT TO DO NEXT! What did we LEARN? There is ALWAYS SOMETHING MORE TO LEARN! The POSITIVE mindset DOESN'T get into a CIRCUMSTANTIAL CAB and say… 'Just DRIVE! Take me ANYWHERE! It DOESN'T MATTER!'

It most certainly DOES MATTER! How can we expect our LIVES to get any better is we were to just ROLL OVER or THROW our HANDS UP and SURRENDER. Allowing the 'NEGATIVE' dark forces of PEOPLE, PLACES and SITUATIONS to have VICTORY over our LIVES. When DEEP down inside we know that OUR PURPOSE in LIFE has so MUCH MORE.

A POSITIVE MINDSET will erect a COLLATERAL DAMAGE RECOVERY plan when LIFE'S dramas and tragedies come. We don't just EVACUATE and ISOLATE. We may have to make a TACTICAL RETREAT from UNHEALTHY THINKING and SITUATIONS. For the SOLE PURPOSE of making a PROFOUND COMEBACK!

- SIGNS OF A POSITIVE MINDSET

First of all of all we don't 'LOOK LIKE… WHAT WE'VE BEEN THROUGH!' There is an ever abiding presence of PEACE, JOY and CONTENTMENT. These are the FRUIT that grows when a SOUL has found and probably FOUGHT our way through so many CHALLENGES. We are the BLESSED ONES that KNOW that in due time all will be well. Our SPIRITUAL CONNECTION has been fortified with the experiences that there is a LOVING POWER that is far greater than ANY of US! And has every bit of the same capacity to LOOK OVER, LEAD, GUIDE and PROTECT US as we follow the WISDOMS that LIFE GIVES.

We don't draw back with DEFEAT at FAILED ATTEMPTS of projects and personal ventures. We LIVE and LEARN! YES… We feel the pains of DISAPPOINTMENTS like everyone else DOES. I PROMISE... if you CUT US, WE WILL BLEED! But HEAVEN forbid that we should just stand there in a SELF-SORRY MODE and continue to BLEED and DO NOTHING.

A POSITIVE SENSE of SELF recovers with greater tenacity in the FEAR of DIFFICULTY and TRIALS. If POSITIVITY would take on a VISIBLE PHYSICAL form it would first of be made of CORK. YES... CORK! When the FLOODS of LIFE come RAGING IN. We may temporarily GO UNDER. But just like a 'CORK' the further DOWN we GO. The HIGHER we RISE on our way back up.

It's even apparent in our 'TRYING DAYS. With our 'HAPPY-GO-LUCKY SELVES. Smiling PEACEFULLY and CONTENTLY going about our business except on a day when we are at a low level of JOY. Our SMILE not as WIDE as usual. Then someone will say... 'Hey! You ALRIGHT?! Don't see that BIG SMILE that you usually have?' They have become so accustomed to our normally VIBRANT spirit that when we are down it draws IMMEDIATE ATTENTION. Difference being that we have allowed our FEELINGS to EXPRESS THEMSELVES.

But we don't consent to OUR FEELINGS grabbing our 'EMOTIONAL STEERING WHEEL'. And driving us to MENTAL STATES that are NOT HEALTHY and where we DON'T WANT to GO! We have uncommon 'BOUNCE BACK'. POSITIVITY keeps us LEVEL-HEADED and STABLE to maintain our EMOTIONAL BALANCE.

EMOTIONAL BALANCE is CRUCIAL to individuals and relationships. There has been many crimes committed in the 'HEAT OF PASSION'. When someone was completely DISTORTED and NOT themselves due to OUT OF CONTROL EMOTIONS!

- CONTENMENT

We've all heard it said... 'THAT I CAN DO BAD... ALL BY MYSELF!' OK! But what about... 'DOING GOOD... ALL BY YOURSELF?' CONTENTMENT is that state of everything is alright... RIGHT NOW. Not WAITING, WANTING or depending on some GREAT EVENT to take place so that LIFE can have a FULLER MEANING! CONTENTMENT is that tangible evidence that YOU are HEALTHY, WHOLE and FIT for the SINGLE, DATING and MARRIED LIFE! It's an ONGOING WORK in PROGRESS. Allow yourself the wonderful privilege to REACH and GO HIGHER for a DEEPER sense of INNER PEACE and OUTER INTERACTIONS that will BLESS and BENEFIT YOU... and OTHERS!

Like the prayer that says... "Give me enough RICHES where I will NOT become ARROGANT and THINK that I don't need GOD. Or NOT have enough and I become a THEIF who STEALS and EMBARRASSES GOD!" Many of us have not allowed ourselves to develop to where we don't FEEL like a WHOLE PERSON. And a relationship with SOMEONE ELSE will COMPLETE US... and make US WHOLE. CONTENTMENT builds us up from within and BINDS all of our INNER PIECES TOGETHER to create in US as ONE DYNAMIC SOUL. Who is NOW READY to... 'DO GOOD with A SIGNIFICANT OTHER.

- JOY

That unexplainable INNER UPLIFT that transcends SITUATIONS and CIRCUMSTANCES. Not to be CONFUSED with HAPPINESS which comes and goes based on the present APPEALS of our LIFE. When particulars are going in our FAVOR. The person with a POSITIVE MINDSET is the recipient of a 'GLOW' of knowing that LIFE and it's

BLESSINGS are always known and ACCESSIBLE. That NO condition can UNDO or OVERCOME what we have. And WHAT DO WE HAVE?

A SPIRITUAL CONNECTION that is like having our MOST PRECIOUS and LOVED ONES... SURROUNDING, LOVING, PROTECTING and ENJOYING LIFE with US! The VICTORIOUS result is in an EFFERVESCENT HIGH that pronounces our ULTIMATE SATISFACTION. If HAPPINESS were a NICE TWO-SEATER SPORTS CAR. Than JOY would be our STRECTH LIMOUSINE that carries us through life with an EMOTIONAL sense of INNER LUXURY!

JOY maintains it's ENERGETIC UPLIFT even and especially in our most TRYING and DIFFICULT times. This is what makes it's presence so OUTSTANDING to the watching world. They may be aware of our times of HARSH REALITIES we face. But cannot see the USUAL NEGATIVE SIDE-EFFECTS that are commonly expected on US!

JOY comes in as if the TENSIONS and STRESSES of LIFE have been removed and OVERCOME as if they were NEVER PRESENT. Allowing us the very GIFTED PLEASURE to SMILE even through our TEARS!

- PEACE

Don't know whether JOY comes FIRST and then PEACE. Or PEACE comes FIRST and then JOY! But beloved, we do know that they do RIDE and ROLL together. When and WHERE there is the ONE. It won't be long before the other comes right along side.

They are a COMPLIMENTARY CONFIRMATION with each other and to the individual that possess them. PEACE is that very EXTRAORDINARY place that GOD gives our MIND, SPIRIT and EMOTIONS a haven to reside through our STORMS of LIFE.

It's the element of SURRENDERING for the GOOD. No more INNER HEAD-BANGING, trying to fit SQUARE PEGS into ROUND HOLES! Or FRUITLESS JOURNEYS that have no BENEFICIAL DESTINATIONS. We lay down our arms of SELF-CENTERED EFFORTS knowing we are NOT solely dependant upon our OWN RESOURCES. We don't take up ARGUMENTS and BATTLES within OURSELVES or others with RECKLESS ABANDON. PEACE allows WISDOM a comfortable place to interrupt us from our IMPROMPTU and WAYWARD MISADVENTURES!

PEACE like JOY and CONTENTMENT are gifts that come from a POSITIVE MIND! They are the result of SOUND and HEALTHY applications to LIVING WELL and WISELY. PEACE for the SOUL! JOY for our MIND! And CONTENTMENT for our BODY! So... with these MINDSETS before us. The questions are... "WHAT DO YOU BELIEVE?" Please pay close ATTENTION! You may want to take NOTES! There will be many LIFE TESTS!

- DO YOU BELIEVE... "THAT THERE IS SOMEBODY FOR EVERYBODY?"

With statistics about BAD RELATIONSHIPS and the HIGH DIVORCE RATES makes us all wonder. Is it really SOMEONE out there for EVERYONE? I believe that is they have not COME TO US YET. They may have possibly PASSED US BY. Whether WE were AWARE OR NOT! Maybe in HINDSIGHT we can remember a certain SOMEONE that we wished we could have maybe done something differently... NOW. If we ONLY had that CHANCE!

But CHANCE is not a particular SEARCH DEVICE that I would recommend. It has to be a deliberate ACT of WILL, RESEARCH,

DISCERNMENT, DECLARATION and DESIGN! No more FRANTICALLY searching WEB-SITES as if our LIVES depended on it. Just continue to be YOUR BRIGHTEST STAR in the SKY. Where your presence CANNOT and WILL NOT be DENIED. To NOT BELIEVE will drown US in a POOL of TEARS, LONLINESS and SORROW that we can prevent NOW by being OUR BEST and being READY!

- DO YOU BELIEVE... "IN LOVE FOR A LIFETIME?"

Like a popular song back in the 90's that said... "NOW THAT WE'VE FOUND LOVE! What are we going to DO WITH IT?" To those of us that have run down the aisle of SACRED MATRIMONY. Believing that our DREAMBOAT has come and will CARRY US away into the land of HAPPY-EVER-AFTER. Only to be HEART-BROKEN and distraught to find our KNIGHT has lost his GLEAMOR and SHINE. Do we dare continue to BELIEVE that LOVE LIVES for a LIFETIME... AGAIN! Or whether it will come after so many SAD CASES of LOVE gone WRONG.

Is it SAFE and even SMART to LOOK for a LOVEBOAT to finish our CRUISE of LIFE? LOVE is and does last a LIFETIME! What we do with it when it does come is ENTIRELY UP to US! LOVE is the most ETERNAL ELEMENT that is known to MAN. Unfortunately we have not regarded it so. There needs to be a much keener PERSPECTIVE on this AWESOME gift that has been given to our disposal. It becomes a LIFE GIVING FORCE that BUILDS and BINDS individuals through the years. It actually has the capacity to add YOUTH and YEARS to LIFE. And reverberates even beyond DISTANCE, RACIAL LINES and even the GRAVE!

- DO YOU BELIEVE... "IT'S POSSIBLE TO STAY FAITHFUL?"

INFIDELITY is PROBABLY the SINGLE MOST CONCERNED issue in all relationships. FIDELITY is a concerted effort that requires UNCOMPROMISING COMMITMENT... EVERYDAY. I was trying my best to reserve this particular discourse for the ending HEART MESSAGES. But I need to lay this OUT HERE and NOW!

We have been SOLD a SORRY BILL of GOODS! We have been INTENTIONALLY and OVERLY EXPOSED to view HUMAN BEINGS as MERCHANDISE for all our SELFISH NEEDS. More so than any other is this so APPARENT (...and I might add, RAMPANT) than in the areas of SEXUAL EXPLOITATION! We need to see beyond the VEILS of ALLURMENT and ENTICEMENT. And WAKE UP to the SYSTEMATIC STRATEGY that we are being DUPED from within. Outside entities are paying multiple thousands (...if not MILLIONS) to seek out what's INSIDE our HEADS!

What is the next ADVERTISING CONTRAPTION and PUBLICITY SCHEME to be created and used against us? For the sake of making MULTIPLIED RICHES for others from our LUST-FILLED DESIRES? What do I say to this? Advertisers devise intricate ways to make us feel DISSATISFIED and INCOMPLETE with what we HAVE. We need a NEW THIS! A NEW MODEL THAT! Well SEX MERCHANDISERS are well aware of the successful formulas that sell anything from CARS to HYPER-GENIC SOAP.

Our natural GOD-GIVEN desires are put on an OPEN FLAME of UNREPENTANT excess which is MIND-BLOWING. This creates DESIRES that are UNNATURAL and what was NEVER intended for the MENTAL and EMOTIONAL BENEFIT of MEN and WOMEN. This is the NEW FRUIT that continues to plague our society that first struck

ADAM and EVE in the garden of Eden. Too much KNOWLEDGE in the hands of the unprepared LEADS to DISATER... EVERY TIME!

- SO WHAT DO WE DO TO INSURE OUR FIDELITY IN RELATIONSHIPS?

FIRST and FOREMOST we must ACCEPT and RECOGNIZE what is HEALTHY and what is UNHEALTHY! What we should TREASURE and what is GARBAGE! We must FILTER through the FALSE IMPRESSIONS that would have US chasing THRILLING MIRAGES of what WE thought was WATER on a DRY and HOT DESERT.

We have to KNOW OUR PARTNERS and especially OURSELVES. So TRUTHFULLY and WELL enough to BAR and INSULATE those potential DANGERS that will come! One of the most challenging things that MEN will ever face is if an ATTRACTIVE WOMAN wants to be with him. And then let it be made known to a man and even does NOT CARE if he is in a RELATIONSHIP or MARRIED!

I believe that this is the same situation that the BIBLE talks about with JOSEPH when he was tempted by Potipher's wife! *Gen. 39:1-13. YES... Joseph loved GOD and did not want to SIN. But Joseph had to know himself well enough to RUN AWAY QUICKLY! He had to know that if he LINGERED that he would be WEAKENED... and GIVE IN!

We men must KNOW when it's okay to ... RUN AWAY! It's not about trying to search and PROVE how STRONG we can be in the FACE of a FULL-FRONTAL ASSUALT. Especially in an area where we know that we can find PLEASURE. A WISE soldier knows when to make a TACTICAL RETREAT to be able to FIGHT ANOTHER DAY. Yes... women get WEAK also. Giving in to TEMPTATIONS of LUST and SEXUAL EXHILARATIONS.

But the 'DIRT' on NO GOOD MEN is when they WILLINGLY and DECEITFULLY LIE to become RECKLESSLY involved with as many women as he can get his SWEATY HANDS ON. This is a FEAR that impedes many women's PSYCHE. Whether they are in a RELATIONSHIP or NOT and INSECURE about getting into one. "Will my MAN stay TRUE and FAITHFUL?" they say with exasperation. And here's some POSITIVE reasons... HOW and WHY!

- KEYS TO FIDELITY

SUBMISSION is the MAIN INGREDIENT for FIDELITY and HARMONY in RELATIONSHIPS! How so?.... 'JUST DO WHAT WE SAY?!" Unfortunately some men have blatantly tried that MENTALITY and FAILED MISERABLY in building TRUSTING and HEALTHY relations.

Many BIBLE, THUMPING and CHEST-POUNDING men of FAITH have stood on a SOAP BOX and CRIED OUTLOUD... 'WIVES SUBMIT to your own HUSBANDS, as to the LORD." *Eph. 5:22. We know that BIBLE verse and 'JESUS wept" *John 11:35, if we don't know NO OTHER VERSES!

Whereas many modern day women will unapologetically OPPOSE this verse as being IRREVERANT, IRRELAVENT and OUTDATED. That this particular BIBLE verse was for a period of an UNCILIVILIZED MONARCHY. Where men ruled with an IRON FIST and a TIGHT GRIP.

I see that SUBMISSION is a POWERFUL tool for the woman to play a CRUCIAL role in AFFIRMING the MAN in HER LIFE! HOW? Here's what I have discovered about a woman of FAITH in SUBMISSION.

SUBMITTING to GOD is very appropriate because HE is LOVING and OMNISCIENT. The MAN is intended to emulate the LOVING and KNOWING characteristics of GOD. We can blindly follow GOD's lead because we have CONFIDENCE that in the end it will all work out for our GOOD! However MAN is not GOD and is very limited in many ways.

I have heard many times over that a women's quandary in following MEN is that… "What if where he LEAD's ain't RIGHT? Or I don't AGREE WITH?" Very UNDERSTANDABLE and REASONABLE! Now here's my UNDERSTANDING! When a woman SUBMITS to her MAN or MATE this is very STRIKING, APPRECIATED and COMFORTING. This sends the message to MEN that his LEADERSHIP is TRUSTED. TRUST here is the KEY!

When a MAN has your TRUST even in the face of your varying or DIFFERENT OPINIONS and BELIEFS. This AGREEMENT provides the MAN with a PLACE of COMFORT between HIM and YOU… my dear SISTERS. The place of COMFORT that YOU provided HIM through your SUBMISSION is now a PLACE where you can meet him and have FREE DISCUSSION.

When there is OPPOSITION at the point of INITIAL EXPRESSION the result is that WALLS GO UP and the DEFENSES are LED IN! When a military leader provides a STRATEGIC plan he shares this and expects these plans to be ACCEPTED. His expectation goes by the CHAIN of COMMAND down to the troops. RESISTANCE will cause ANARCHY within the ranks and ultimately this will lead to MILITARY TRAGEDY and DEFEAT!

RELATIONSHIPS are not like the MILITARY. But the example was to demonstrate the importance of the LEADERS need for POSITIONAL RESPECTABILITY. When the LEADERS place is ACKNOWLEGED and given it's proper STATURE, there will be EFFECTIVE relations. No structure of any personnel can function without someone UNDERGIRDING… WHO and WHAT is in CHARGE.

In relationships this is not a LESSER or GREATER than SCENARIO. MEN are NOT (… I REPEAT, NOT!) inherently better than WOMEN and WOMEN are NOT SO over MEN! It's all about FUNCTION. ONE CAR! ONE STEERING WHEEL! There can be many QUALIFIED PASSENGERS WITH approved LISCENSE, EXCELLENT DRIVING SKILLS and EXPERIENCE. But ALL CANNOT DRIVE… at the SAME TIME!

The designated driver uses his WISDOM for the sake of all when FATIGUE or LOSS of DIRECTION comes into play. He then enlists the assistance of SOMEONE else to DRIVE in his stead. He KNOWS that it's NOT up to HIM to DIRECTLY try to DO EVERYTHANG! So he SUBMITS and relinquishes his TASK without any LOSS of his IDENTITY.

So to does the MAN who SUBMITS to his WELL QUALIFIED MATE in their different areas of LIVING. SUBMISSION now comes and GOES FULL CIRCLE. The MAN NOW… SUBMITS and displays the SAME TRUST to HER that SHE does to HIM. TRUE SUBMISSION BUILDS… NEVER DIVIDES.

So…? How does SUBMISSION become a relevant factor in FIDELITY? When couples are engaged in SEXUAL INTIMACY, there is a constant ONGOING SUBMISSION to one another! NOTICE… I said 'SEXUAL INTIMACY' and NOT SEXUAL ACTIVITY! There's a WORLD of DIFFERENCE. When there is SEXUAL INTIMACY there is a UNIQUE

ENERGY that exists between them. The resulting CHEMISTRY is I dare say … the AFTER-EFFECT.

It's this ENERGETIC AFTER-EFFECT that lingers with the MAN and WOMAN that many, unfortunately not even aware of. This AWESOME ENERGY LIVES ON well after the LOVEMAKING has been lovingly placed in the ROMANTIC MEMOIRS. This SUBMISSIVE ENERGY that is passed between LOVERS can also be called upon in moments of TEMPTATION and DIFFERENCES of OPINIONS that we may have. When we LEAVE this ENTITY only for the BEDROOM. We have DERAILED a LIFE ENERGY that is intended to be a MAJOR INGREDIENT in the BONDING process of the TWO becoming ONE!

For US MEN we have to SUBMIT to a TRANSFORMED MENTALITY in regard to WOMEN as a WHOLE! What creates these LUST-FILLED APPETITES for us? It's when we view OTHER WOMEN as POTENTIAL LOVERS. Example? I have four BEAUTIFUL and OUTSTANDING daughters named JOVAN, PHOENICIA, NINA and KEYANA. (Yes… I named all four of them!) When I see YOUNGER WOMEN and when there would be a TEMPTING thought to MENTALLY UNDRESS them. I've LEARNED and PRACTICED to SEE them in the same LIGHT as I would my DAUGTHERS.

So there is an INSTANT DOSING of TRANSFORMED, COLD-WATER THINKING that DRENCHES any LUST-FILLED DESIRES. So now I can LOOK without the 'LUSTING'! YES!... It takes and TOOK PRACTICE! We have been BRAIN WASHED into believing that… "It's OKAY to LOOK!" That can and very EASILY DOES lead to wanting MORE than just LOOKING! Which becomes then the 'HOOK' that CATCHES US!"

That initial process of SUBMITTING with our LOVED ONE helps a MAN create a MIND SET of AFFIRMATIVE SUBMISSION. Where it is not looked upon within himself as a LESSER STATE of MANHOOD. It in fact becomes a SUBSTANTIAL ASSET to our NEW FOUND MALE INTEGRITY and IDENTITY. FAITHFULNESS becomes a BADGE of HONOR and a GREAT SOURCE of PRIDE for those MATURE MEN that LIVE this way ... DAILY!

- WILLINGNESS

All the PRAYING, RELATIONSHIP and MARRIAGE SEMINARS in the world won't do a BIT OF GOOD. In being FAITHFUL if there isn't the WILLINGNESS to do so. FAITHFULNESS is a DAILY CREED and DECLARATION to be SINGLEY and EXCLUSIVELY for ONE PERSON... PERIOD!

Yes... like the R&B group HEATWAVE sang so heartfelt on their late 70's hit song... 'ALWAYS and FOREVER'! That means particularly for MEN, a MENTAL and EMOTIONAL RE-ARRANGING of our ERRONEOUS ZONES. A complete 'WIPING THE SLATE'! No leftover memoirs from 'HOT FLASHES' of HEATED ENCOUNTERS of the CLOSE KIND!

But a FULL TRANSITIONING from a MAN in 'HOT PURSUIT' to a MAN pursuing the SATISFACTIONS of 'LOVE'. We MEN spend so much THOUGHT, TIME and ENRGY chasing that elusive 'PERFECT WOMAN' only to find our motors REVVING UP at the SIGHT and THOUGHT of the next episode of 'RUN, RUN, RUN!' The ironic part of MEN CHASING women, is that NO WOMAN will ever match the 'PERFECT' fantasy woman that so many MEN are CAPTIVATED by.

She's NOT REAL! We have only imagined her to be everything in BED that we want her to be. And then absolutely just RIGHT as she caters to all our VERTICAL needs as well. When this DISAPPOINTED REALITY sets in. For some reason we MEN don't see our THINKING PROCESS as being FLAWED. But some MEN unfairly attributes WOMEN to BLAME that are in all aspects probably better than we have EVALUATED. We MEN would be better served to re-evaluate WOMEN under more ACUTE SCRUTINY than to continue an ASESSMENT that FALLS SHORT and FAILS! Men like WOMEN should persist in believing that the RIGHT PERSON is still out there. SOMEWHERE WITHIN OUR REACH!

It takes an all out EXCLUSIVE WILLINGNESS to deem the woman of our CHOOSING, to be the ONE and ONLY WOMAN for US. NOT IF... SUCH and SUCH happens. And then we are OUTTA HERE! Or worse yet... SNEAKING AROUND! Resisting TEMPTATION actually builds a MAN's character. We just have to admit that we are NOT MISSING something MIND-BLOWING! This means that even if we're not willing... we still MUST BE! HOW?

PRAY! Pray the 'HUMILITY PRAYER! GOD... Please! HELP ME, HELP YOU, HELP ME!" I've learned through my many LIFE JOURNEYS, STRUGGLES and CHALLENGES... that GOD can do for me what I find IMPOSSIBLE for me to do for MYSELF!

In other words... GET OUT OF YOUR OWN WAY! I believe it's the EMOTIONAL MAKE-UP of women that applies so much PRESSURE on them to do right that it SWAYS them in a way where man are still EMOTIONALLY STUNTED. So our EMOTIONAL CALLOUSNESS keeps our EMOTIONAL SELVES from intervening on our conscious to DO THE RIGHT THING! We are more driven by our SEX IMPULSES that pushes our conscious to the back wall of our MIND and tells it to stay there... and BE QUIET!

We must allow a SUPREME WILLINGNESS over our DESIRE for a FANTASY SEXCAPADE from invading our MINDS and leading us into the FAÇADE of INFIDELITY. And that is the GIFT of the INDOMITABLE SPIRIT! The UNCONQUERABLE SOUL! This is WHY we still exist as a people today. Unfortunately WE are a PEOPLE where many are DIVIDED. So... Make the DIFFERENCE wherever YOU ARE! YOU are the DIFFERENCE! The DIFFERENCE IS YOU!

This is the BELIEF that will OUTLIVE US ALL! This PRECIOUS gift of the ETERNAL SPIRIT that has been passed down to US! Many of us are TOTALLY UNAWARE of these TRUTHS and our lives are EMPTY SHELLS of what they are INTENDED to BE!

KEEP YOUR HEAD UP! KNOW the TRUTH! KNOW what to do... EVEN WHEN YOU DON'T KNOW... WHAT to DO! LEAD the WAY! Let GOD LEAD YOU! BELIEVE that HE WILL... and I being HIS LIVING WITNESS! I SAY to YOU... that HE WILL! BELIEVE that and YOU will live ABDUNDANTLY as well as EVERYONE under your CARE. And this is WHAT and WHY... WE WILL ALWAYS BELIEVE!

*MESSAGE FROM THE HEART!

LISTENING to the MEN may be very CHALLENGING for some. TRUST ISSUES can cast a DARK SHADOW if it's ALLOWED. Believing that YOU may ALREADY know what's about to be SAID before... it's SAID! It's not a question of INTELLIGENCE. It's all about respecting APPLIED WISDOM!

KNOWING what to DO and WHY ... is the KEY to better UNDERSTANDING. No one can BEST UNDERSTAND a MAN than other MEN. We share what we THINK... because WOMEN cannot THINK... like A MAN! But can certainly UNDERSTAND a MAN'S THOUGHT!

The ability to originate a MALE THOUGHT is not in the capability of WOMEN!

Likewise we MEN need to understand a WOMEN'S MENTALITY because we do no GENERATE FEMALE IDEAS. So UNDERSTANDING is the MAKE or BREAKING POINTS. Our BRIDGE is built on MUTUAL WILLINGNESS to want to DO and BE BETTER!

When we can AGREE to AGREE. And AGREE to DISAGREE! We will find that we won't get confounded in DISAGREEING to DISAGREE! RESPECT allows us to comfortably be who we are as we let others BE WHO THEY ARE. All with their OPINIONS, BELIEFS and INDIVIDUAL IDENTITIES all INTACT!

These are the many LIFE LESSONS that I have LEARNED throughout my LIFE JOURNEY. Not having a FATHER to raise me to MANHOOD. Enduring ABUSE at an EARLY AGE! ADOLESCENT LONLINESS and DEPRESSION! IDENTITY and SELF-ESTEEM challenges! UNHAPPILY MARRIED for years! ADDICTIONS! HOMELESSNESS! And BANKRUPTCY have all molded my FAITH and my CORE BEING to want to share with others the story of TRUE WISDOM and VICTORY!

Not being FAMOUS, RICH, CELEBRITY or a PROFESSIONAL ATHLETE. I have written these words with the INSPIRED WISDOM that GOD has given me to share with YOU! Can't even begin to tell you how many days I sat writing. And were receiving WHAT TO SAY... at the VERY MOMENT that I WAS WRITING!

The POWER of these writings come from the TRUTH that is contained in them. I have journeyed down pathways that only a few of us have TREAD and OVERCAME! Many like myself have STRUGGLED and found SUCCESS through our DECISIONS to change our course for the

ULTIMATE GOOD! GOOD for OURSELVES and GOOD for EVERYONE that GOD sends our way!

So I take great PRIDE and am privileged to speak words of HEALTH, HEALING and WHOLENESS in this realm of RELATIONSHIPS! To share this LITERARY LOVE from one who is among the MASSES of like-minded MEN. Such a VITAL ISSUE! Our RELATIONSHIPS with OURSELVES and OTHERS will determine the WORLD that we and our CHILDREN'S, CHILDREN'S, CHILDREN will live in.

- So what are WE GOING TO DO ABOUT IT?

Will we even LISTEN to CONSIDER what TRUTH we have to SAY? Or will we just do like so many other generations long before us and SAY.... "WE WILL HEAR THIS MATTER ANOTHER DAY!"

"I PRAY that... WE WILL HAVE EARS TO HEAR!"

*GOD puts our lives together like a PUZZLE. One PIECE at a TIME! Every piece is a VERY IMPORTANT PART that connects the WHOLE VISION for our LIVES."

Printed in the United States
By Bookmasters